CONCISE INDEX TO ENGLISH

EUGENE EHRLICH
DANIEL MURPHY

McGraw-Hill Book Company
New York • St. Louis • San Francisco • London • Düsseldorf
Kuala Lumpur • Mexico • Montreal • Panama • São Paulo
Sydney • Toronto • Johannesburg • New Delhi • Singapore

Copyright © 1974 by McGraw-Hill, Inc. All rights reserved. Printed in the United States of America. No part of this publication may be reproduced, stored in a retrieval system, or transmitted, in any form or by any means, electronic, mechanical, photocopying, recording, or otherwise, without the prior written permission of the publisher.

"Poem 271" copyright, 1935, by e. e. cummings; renewed, 1963, by Marion Morehouse Cummings. Reprinted from *Complete Poems 1913-1962* by e. e. cummings by permission of Harcourt Brace Jovanovich, Inc.

23456789MUMU7987654

Library of Congress Cataloging in Publication Data

Ehrlich, Eugene H
  Concise Index to English.

  (McGraw-Hill paperbacks)
  1. English language--Grammar--1950- --Handbooks, manuals, etc. I. Murphy, Daniel Joseph, 1921- joint author. II. Title.
PE1106.E4   808   74-542
ISBN 0-07-019101-8

PREFACE

We have attempted to fulfill certain responsibilities in compiling this book. Above all, we wanted to supply authoritative answers to questions asked most often by writers and students of writing. Secondly, we wanted our readers to find desired answers as easily as possible and to understand those answers readily. Finally, we hoped that our readers would not be bored or oppressed by what they read whenever they sought help in this book.

Concise Index to English, therefore, presents alphabetically certain principles, precepts, practices, and prejudices in matters of syntax and style. And it does so as directly as possible.

We leave to our readers the final word on whether we have served them faithfully.

E. E.
D. M.

ACKNOWLEDGMENT

The authors wish to thank Richard Ehrlich for his assistance in critically reading the manuscript of *Concise Index to English*.

Dedicated to the memory of Danny Murphy Jr., son of Daniel and Eileen Murphy.

A

ABBREVIATION

While abbreviations are permissible in informal writing—personal letters, class notes, stories using familiar language—they should be used sparingly in papers or documents requiring formal English. In footnotes and bibliographies, abbreviations are used extensively. Abbreviations are most appropriate in publications in which space is at a premium: business reports, manuals, and reference books. The best example of a publication in which space is at a premium is a telephone directory.

Commonly Used Abbreviations Mr., Mrs., Dr., M.D., B.A., and Ph.D. are commonly used with names: Mrs. James Jackson, B.A.; Alfred Nieman, M.D. We never write, "He is a Dr.," since an abbreviation is not used to designate a group or class. Names of familiar agencies (S.E.C. and C.I.A.) are usually abbreviated, and the periods within the abbreviations may be omitted (SEC and CIA). A.D., B.C., etc., a.m., and p.m. are almost never given except as abbreviations. When used with a name, Professor and other titles are abbreviated if the first name or initials of the person are supplied: Professor Hughes, Prof. E. F. Fairchuck, Reverend Wilkins, Rev. T. S. Wilkins. The abbreviation Ms. is coming into use now to designate a woman without reference to her marital status. This designation has the appearance of an abbreviation, but one does not know what it stands for.

Scholarly Abbreviations English has many abbreviations for words used frequently in scholarly writing, particularly in bibliographic entries.

[1] Cleanth Brooks and Robert Penn Warren, *Modern Rhetoric*, 2nd. ed. (New York, 1949), p. 47.
[2] Thomas Mann, *The Holy Sinner*, trans. H. T. Lowe-Porter (New York, 1951), p. 9.
[3] *Ibid.*, p. 94.

The trend in scholarly writing is to avoid using abbreviations. In any formal writing, therefore, with the exception of certain scholarly journals, these abbreviations should not be used, since many readers do not know the meanings intended. If you are going to use abbreviations in your documentation of formal papers or articles, you should be familiar with the most common abbreviations:

Abbreviation	Latin Meaning	Meaning
c., ca.	circa	about or around (referring to dates or time)
cf.	confer	compare
cm.		centimeter
ed.		editor, edition, edited by
e.g.	exempli gratia	for example
et al.	et alii, et alios	and others
et seq.	et sequens	and the following
f., ff.		the following page, pages
fig.		figure
ibid.	ibidem	in the same place
i.e.	id est	that is
il., illus.		illustration, illustrated by
loc. cit.	loco citato	in the place cited
MS, MSS		manuscript, manuscripts
n.d.		no date given
n.s.		new series
No.		number
op. cit.	opere citato	in the work cited
p., pp.		page, pages
q.v.	quod vide	which see
rev.		revised, revised by
s.		series
sup.		supplement, supplements
tr.		translation, translated by
vol., vols.		volume, volumes

Two other terms used by scholars deserve mention here even though they are not abbreviations: *passim*—in different sections of a text cited without specific reference to pages; and *sic*—thus—which signifies that material has been quoted correctly even though it appears to contain an error. *Sic* is always enclosed in brackets.

Dictionaries may supply abbreviations in a special list, as entries in the main listing following the word abbreviated, or as separate entries. When in doubt about an abbreviation, consult the dictionary.

Periods with Abbreviations   Except in special cases, listed below, abbreviations are followed by periods.

- Periods are frequently omitted in the abbreviations for government agencies, labor unions, airlines, and the like—FBI, TWA, CBS, AFL-CIO.
- Acronyms, abbreviations pronounced as words, are not punctuated—Wac, UNESCO, radar, loran.

The best advice about whether to abbreviate is: *When in doubt, spell it out.*

ADJECTIVE

An adjective is a word used to modify, limit, or describe another word or group of words performing a noun function. Adjectives modify subjects, objects, objects of prepositions, gerunds, and noun clauses:

- The *stone* wall was built to conform with the *oval* shape of the drive.
- The *glaring* lights blinded the driver of the *speeding* car.
- The *red, green,* and *blue* hat perched on her head.

Someone once said that adjectives are the death of nouns. What this means is that a great deal of uneven and careless writing results from the excessive use of adjectives. A precise word does not need adjectives.

Comparison of Adjectives   Adjectives can be cast in forms that reflect degrees of the characteristic being communicated. This is done by adding *er* or *est* to the positive form or by placing *more* or *most* before the positive form.

Positive	*Comparative*	*Superlative*
friendly	friendlier	friendliest
friendly	more friendly	most friendly

Position of Adjectives   An adjective may occur before or after the noun it modifies. In simple modification the adjective usually precedes the noun.

- *small* pony, *rigid steel* structure, *open* door

Adjectives can follow the word modified (1) in order to achieve emphasis, (2) because of a pattern inherited from another language, or (3) because the adjective is itself modified, and placing it before the word modified would be awkward.

Emphasis

the tour *complete* for twenty-four dollars

The country, *divided*, was on the verge of civil war.

Pattern from Another Language

attorney *general*, court-*martial*, secretary-*general*

Adjective Modified

a design so *intricate*, a plan infinitely *complex* (*so* modifies *intricate*, *infinitely* modifies *complex*)

ADVERB

An adverb modifies verbs, adjectives, and other adverbs.

- He hit the ball *sharply*.

A better choice of verb would eliminate the adverb.

- He *smashed* the ball. He *whacked* the ball. He *pounded* the ball.

Form of Adverbs Most adverbs end in *ly*, but a handful—derived mainly from Old English—do not have any special adverbial sign: *now, quite, then, there, when, yes,* and *no*.

Comparison of Adverbs Most adverbs show degrees of comparison by adding *er* or *est*, or by placing *more* or *most* before the adverb. (See ADJECTIVE for discussion of degrees of comparison.)

Identifying Adverbs in a Sentence A simple formula identifies adverbs and adverbial phrases and clauses in a sentence:

$$\text{verb} + \begin{cases} \text{when?} \\ \text{where?} \end{cases} \begin{array}{l} \text{why?} \\ \text{how?} \\ \text{how much?} \end{array}$$

- With the same bat, the shortstop yesterday smashed the ball out of the park.

The verb is *smashed*:

- Smashed how? *with the same bat*
- Smashed when? *yesterday*
- Smashed where? *out of the park*

If there were more room in the sentence, we might also have answered smashed why?—to boost his batting average.

Position of Adverbs   Adverbs and adverbial constructions have no fixed position in an English sentence. Single-word adverbs should be placed as closely as possible to the word or group of words they modify.

- She *certainly* failed.
- The boat crashed *heavily* on the rocks.
- He *almost* finished the examination.

Adverbial phrases and clauses precede or follow the main statement; however, the order in which these modifiers are placed can vary, as in these five versions of the same sentence:

- *Before the woman could reach the door,* the rain splashed *furiously around her.*
- *Before the woman could reach the door,* the rain splashed *around her furiously.*
- The rain splashed *furiously around the woman before she could reach the door.*
- The rain splashed *around the woman furiously before she could reach the door.*
- *Around the woman* the rain splashed *furiously before she could reach the door.*

[AD]

When you are trying different sentence patterns in your writing, remember that adverbial constructions can be moved rather freely to enable you to achieve the rhythm and flow desired.

AFFECT, EFFECT

The simplest means of distinguishing between these troublesome words is to remember that *effect* is normally a noun meaning a *result, affect* a verb meaning *influence.*

- The *effect* of the experiment encouraged the scientists.
- The accident did not *affect* the result of the race.

In formal English, *effect* is used as a verb meaning *to bring about,* usually in the passive.

- The result *was effected* by several means.

This use of *effect* as a verb is overdone in scientific and technical writing, thus contributing to the weakness and dullness of much of this writing. Writers would do well to rediscover the verb *cause* and try using it whenever they are inclined to use *effect* as a verb.

AGREEMENT

Of all the syntactical problems that plague the writer, agreement is one of the most annoying. (Can problems of agreement be so widespread because logic is becoming so rare in daily life?) Yet questions of agreement can always be resolved by resorting to logical analysis of what is intended in a sentence.

Subject and Verb   Subject and verb must agree in number—when a subject is singular, its verb must also be singular; when a subject is plural, its verb must also be plural.

- The *man wants* to do the best job he can.
- Most *men have returned* home by nightfall.
- The *criterion is* success in life.
- *Formulas exist* for solving most of those problems.

Be careful that agreement is sustained when dealing with a plural subject following a linking verb. Remember that the verb agrees with its *subject*, not with its *subjective complement.*

- *Prudence is* the heart and soul of his nature.
- The *heart* and *soul* of his nature *are* prudence.

If this construction appears awkward, avoid it. In fact, nothing much is added to this thought by coupling *soul* with *heart.* The two words do have separate meanings, but not as they are used in this sentence. Writers are prone to use couplings of this kind—called compound subjects—when a single word will do as well. The agreement of a verb with its subject rather than with its subjective complement is better illustrated by using a real coupling of subjects:

- *Honesty* and *forthrightness* of expression *are* the hallmark of the frontiersman.
- *Ham* and *eggs is* a favorite at the American breakfast table. (Yet, *eggs* and *ham* are staples of the American diet. Here we are not thinking of ham and eggs as a single dish, but of eggs and ham as two different foods.)

Up to this point in the discussion, we have dealt with agreement in simple sentences. Complex sentences introduce another element of difficulty. The number of the subject of a relative clause determines the number of the verb of the relative clause.

- May is one of our teachers *who have contributed* to learned journals.

The inference drawn from this sentence is that May is not the only one of our teachers who have contributed to learned journals. The subject of the relative clause is *who,* and the antecedent of *who* is *teachers.* Since *teachers* is plural, *who* must be plural. Therefore, the verb must be *have contributed,* a plural. This is clear when we rewrite the sentence:

- Of our teachers who have contributed to learned journals, May is one. (Of course, we would never write the sentence this way except to test agreement.)

[AG]

Now consider this sentence:

- May is the only one of our teachers *who has contributed* to learned journals. (Here the antecedent of *who* is *one*. We could rewrite this sentence as: Of our teachers May is the only one who has contributed to learned journals.)

When the parts of a subject are joined by *or* or *nor,* the verb agrees in number and person with the subject closest to it.

- Either he or I *am* to blame.
- Neither the mathematician nor the physicist *is* ready to disclose the findings of the experiment.
- Neither she nor her sisters *are* going to the party.

Pronoun and Antecedent   A pronoun must agree with its antecedent in gender, number, and person—a concept demonstrated partially in the above sentences dealing with the teacher who writes for learned journals.

- The boys are anxious about *their* fair.
- The generals, who were not consulted, now find *themselves* shouldering all the blame.
- Danny will find out that, despite all the support the other boys are giving, *his* opinion will not be honored.
- *What* you will find is that most of your class will be fast asleep by the time you have completed your lecture. (*What* is singular because its antecedent is *that most of your class will be fast asleep by the time you have completed your lecture.*)

Problems arise when pronoun and antecedent are widely separated in a sentence or when one or more words might logically be referred to. By analyzing a sentence grammatically, these faults can be corrected.

- The problems he habitually left for solution early in the morning when a cup of coffee seemed to fortify his first rush of energy with the desire to work were *those* involving calculus. (Not *that.*)

Another problem involves the use of pronouns such as *each, another, anyone, somebody,* and *everybody.* These words are all singular and require a singular pronoun.

- Everybody wants *his* own way in the affair.
- Anyone who is of age can vote for *his* favorite candidate.

The pronoun *none,* which is also singular, is under constant pressure. Consider the following situation:

- Ten member nations are expected to send delegates to a meeting of the World Health Organization. Because of an international crisis, however, all stayed away.

In reporting this incident, do you write:

- None of them attend the meeting.
- None of them attends the meeting.

While *none* is as singular as anything can be—after all, it means *not one,* and *one* is singular—all but the strictest of grammarians would say *none attend*! By now *none* as a singular has practically lost the battle. We are reduced to a situation in which we can insist on a puristic stand and risk sounding stuffy in many cases, or we can go along with the times, or we can avoid the construction.

ALLITERATION

Alliteration is the term used to denote the deliberate repetition of similar consonant sounds. The repetition of sounds for artistic effect is practiced mainly in poetry, but it can be used effectively in prose as well.

> When to the *s*essions of *s*weet *s*ilent thought
> I *s*ummon up remembrance of things past,
> I *s*igh the lack of many a thing I sought....
>
> —Shakespeare, Sonnet XXX

> The *f*air *b*reeze *b*lew, the white *f*oam *f*lew,
> The *f*urrow *f*ollowed *f*ree....
>
> —Coleridge, *Rime of the Ancient Mariner*

> ●*K*indly and *c*lear-sighted ... un*c*ontaminated by their *s*qualor and *c*onfusion, *c*ourageous and firm in his *c*lear allegiances amid the flu*x* of things, a pale angel at the *C*arnival ....
>
> —Santayana, "Dickens"

ALL RIGHT

This is the correct spelling. *Alright, allright,* and *all-right* are all wrong!

AMBIGUITY

A sentence that can be understood in more than one way is ambiguous, an undesirable situation which should be remedied by rewriting. Ask yourself, what am I talking about? Make what you are writing about the subject of your sentence. Then ask, what am I predicating about it? Make that the main verb. In this way the logical and grammatical subjects coincide, and the logical and grammatical verbs coincide.

AMOUNT, NUMBER

Amount is used for things thought of in bulk, *number* for things counted:

- the *amount* of gas, tea, or wood used
- the *number* of lamps, pens, plywood panels sold

AMPERSAND

The ampersand (&) is primarily a space-saving device, used appropriately in informal business writing and reference works. If you are quoting, you must use the ampersand if the original uses it.

AND

And has three principal functions: to link independent clauses; to connect parallel constructions (adjectives, adverbs, nouns, verbs, verbals, phrases, and clauses); and to indicate the last element in

Independent Clauses   When used to join two independent clauses, *and* is always preceded by a comma.

- He decided to go fishing, and Norma said she would go along to watch.

Parallel Structure   *And* connects any two similar grammatical units.

- black and white print, pen and pencil
- the man who likes to write and to talk
- whatever pleased his senses and whatever shocked them

Series   *And*, preceded by a comma, is used before the last element in a series. Although many newspapers, magazines, and much informal writing have stopped using the comma before *and*, formal writing retains it.

Formal   There is no feeling for adventure, romantic love, and sentimentality.

Informal   There is no feeling for adventure, romantic love and sentimentality.

Incorrect Use of AND   Poor writing often uses *and* as a connective where none is needed or where another connective would be more suitable.

Poor   None of the elective courses seemed attractive, and no one registered for them. (Although these two clauses are independent grammatically, they are closely related as to cause and effect.)

Improved   Since none of the elective courses seemed attractive, no one registered for them.

Poor   The sales manager offered no bonuses to salesmen, and his competitors did.

Improved   The sales manager offered no bonuses to salesmen, but his competitors did. Although the sales manager did not offer bonuses.... Although his competitors offered bonuses....

The word *and* is often used incorrectly as the first word of a

[AN]   11

sentence. Although a sentence can open with any word, in formal writing *and* or other coordinating conjunctions are used to open sentences only to achieve a deliberate stylistic effect.

- No solution seemed possible. And Harry knew it.
- No solution seemed possible, and Harry knew it.

ANTECEDENT

An antecedent is the word or group of words to which a pronoun refers.

- Because the *Braddocks* were exhausted, *they* went to sleep. (*Braddocks* is the antecedent of *they*.)
- *John, Fred, and Barry* decided that *they* would go along with the desires of the majority. (*John, Fred, and Barry* is the antecedent of *they*.)

One of the most prevalent faults of beginning writers is their inability to make the antecedent of a pronoun apparent to the reader. The remedy is to keep all pronouns as close as possible to their antecedents, making sure that no word between a pronoun and its antecedent is misconstrued as the antecedent.

- She told Helene that she was not permitted to attend the performance. (Who is not permitted to attend the performance? Only *she* knows, and she is not telling.)

Discovery of this kind of ambiguity sometimes must await a careful reading of a first draft of a paper.

ANTONYM

An antonym is a word that means approximately the opposite of another word.

- hot and cold, black and white, soft and hard

APOSTROPHE

The apostrophe (') is the mark of punctuation used to indicate the possessive case in nouns, the omission of letters in contractions, and dropped letters in reported speech.

Genitives The singular of possessives is formed by adding 's to the base of the word, the plural by adding the apostrophe after the final s.

- a boy's book, a girl's hat, three hours' delay

In the best writing, the apostrophe is used to show possession only for people and time.

Incorrect   the table's legs
Correct   the table legs or the legs of the table

When a name ending in s requires an apostrophe to show possession, add an s after the apostrophe unless the resulting word offends the ear.

- *Yeats's* plays, but not *Euripides's* plays (*Euripides'* plays is far pleasanter.)

Contractions The apostrophe indicates omission of one or more letters in contractions.

- isn't, wouldn't, can't, I'll

The most common error is the confusion of *it's* (meaning *it is*) with *its*, which is the possessive case of *it* and means *belonging to it*.

Reported Speech The apostrophe is used to indicate that certain sounds that ordinarily appear in a word were not spoken:

- "John is goin' and he ain't comin' back," she said.

APPOSITION

Apposition is a construction in which one word or group of words complements or supplements another. When an appositive is restrictive—when it limits the element it complements—it is not punctuated; when it does not limit the element, it is punctuated.

- William the Conqueror (There are many Williams, so *the Conqueror* limits William and is not punctuated.)
- William the Conqueror, King of England and France, is admired even today. (William is already limited by *Conqueror,* so the second appositive, *King of England and France,* is set off by commas.)
- My uncle Ben, who lived in Brooklyn, was a tailor. (The punctuation of this sentence tells us that there is only one uncle Ben in this family, *my* uncle Ben, so *who lived in Brooklyn* is a nonrestrictive appositive.)

ASSONANCE

Assonance is the term used to denote the deliberate repetition of similar vowel sounds. Assonance is used primarily in poetry, but it is also an effective device in prose.

> Therefore a secret unrest
> Tortured thee, brilliant and bold!
> Therefore triumph itself
> Tasted amiss to thy soul.
> Therefore with blood of thy foes,
> Trickled in secret thine own.
>
> —Arnold, *Heine's Grave*

- I cannot forecast to you the action of Russia. It is a riddle wrapped in a mystery inside an enigma.

  —Winston Churchill

ASTERISK

An asterisk (*) is used sometimes to note the presence of a footnote in a paper that has few footnotes. It can also indicate an omission from a quotation or the absence of lines from a quoted poem. In some works asterisks are used to indicate cross references.

ATTRIBUTIVE

An adjective standing next to a noun is attributive.

- the *small* boy
- the man, *passionate* but *disinterested*

Nouns used as adjectives are also attributive.

- the *stone* wall, the *glass* door

AUXILIARY VERB

An auxiliary verb is used with another verb to form tense, mood, or voice.

- The ship *has been* standing in the harbor for days.
- She *will* be happy.
- You *should* go.
- Few parents *are* listened to by their children.

AWKWARD

Awkward is a term applied by critics to writing that is stylistically inadequate. The term indicates that, although no specific rule of grammar has been violated, the writer's message is obscure or ambiguous. The label *awkward* most often means that the writing is loaded with deadwood or marked by illogical word order, sloppy diction, or slack and flabby sentence structure. The remedy is rewriting by searching out all deadwood, correcting faulty diction, and tightening sentence structure. Keep in mind that *direct* writing is seldom awkward: Ask yourself how you would express a given thought if you were asked a direct question by someone standing in front of you. The answer will be direct, and your writing can be just as direct.

B

BE

Be is the most common of all English verbs and the most varied in its forms—*are, was, been,* etc. Writers have no trouble with this verb except for the case of the pronoun that follows *be* when *be* is used as a linking, or copulative, verb. Do we say, "It is I" or "It is me"? The distinction is between the formal and the informal. In the formal we follow *be* with the subjective case, in the informal with the objective.

Informal   it's me, it was him, that's her
Formal   it is I, it was he, that is she

Forms of *be* are used with other verbs to form progressive tenses and to form the passive voice.

- I am walking, I have been walking, they will have been walking
- I was awakened, I had been awakened, they will be awakened

BECAUSE

Because is a subordinating conjunction that gives the reason for the action of the main statement.

- Because we were tired, no one wanted to go.
- The house was torn down, because fire had gutted the entire structure.

Because does not follow such constructions as *the reason is* and *the explanation is.* Instead we say the reason is *that,* the explanation is *that.*

BRACKETS

Brackets ([ ]) are used in formal writing to indicate that some explanation or comment has been added to quoted material.

- Much, however, has been done in the L[ane] matter that should not have been done, and much should be done if only B[lackwell] would lend a hand.
- Should we be per[torn] to go ahead....

If the writer had speculated and filled in the torn section in the previous sentence, that section would have been put into brackets.

- Should we be per[mitted] to go ahead....

Brackets are used with *sic* to indicate that an error in a source is being reproduced exactly.

- Several sources quoted a Pensylvania [sic] study.
- The General Assembly found no dischrepancy [sic] in the revised test.

Brackets are also used in references to enclose material inside parentheses.

- ... and that he had no desire to remain (*The Letters of W. B. Yeats*, ed. Allen Wade [New York, 1955], p. 72).

It is clear, then, that brackets are an *editor's* mark rather than a *writer's* mark. When a writer uses them, he is acting as editor of material he is using in his writing.

BUT

But is used as a coordinating conjunction, as a connective between two grammatically equal units, and as a preposition.

When *but* connects two independent clauses in opposition, it is preceded by a comma.

- Everyone agreed that the party had been a success, but no one wanted to clean up that night.

When *but* connects grammatical units performing similar functions, be certain they are equal—two words, two phrases, or two clauses:

- a virile but gentle man
- ostensibly dancing to the music but actually following an inner rhythm
- He hoped that his wife would go home but that she would rest this time.

When used as a preposition, *but* is not preceded by a comma.

- Everyone wanted to go but Jim.
- We dug for three hours and found nothing but a battered arrowhead.

C

CAPITAL LETTERS

Almost everyone knows that the beginning of a sentence requires a capital letter and that proper names are capitalized, but some confusion exists among students and writers over other uses of capitalization in formal English. The following covers the most common uses for capitalization:

Proper Names Capitalize proper names of persons (Muhammad Ali, John F. Kennedy), places (Oregon, Saskatchewan), races and nationalities (Oriental, Irish), rivers (Hudson, Ohio), days of the week (Friday, Sunday), months (July, September), names of companies (Dow Chemical Company), fraternal organizations (Kiwanis), religious bodies (Church of England), languages (Swahili, French), historical events (Battle of Hastings), and documents (Magna Carta).

Do not capitalize the seasons and the points of the compass. In formal English capitalize the name of a region, despite the fact that most newspapers and some journals tend to use lower case.

- I spent most of my time in Ireland touring the West.

Lines of Verse Capitalize the initial letter of a line of verse unless the poet has not capitalized it himself.

> The sea is calm tonight,
> The tide is full, the moon lies fair
> Upon the Straits;—on the French coast, the light
> Gleams, and is gone; the cliffs of England stand,
> Glimmering and vast, out in the tranquil bay.
> Come to the window, sweet is the night air!
>
> —Arnold, "Dover Beach"

> love is a place
> & through this place of
> love move
> (with brightness of peace)
> all places

[CA]

> yes is a world
> & in this world of
> yes live
> (skilfully curled)
> all worlds
>
> —e. e. cummings, "Poem 271"

Titles of Books, Plays, Articles, Essays, Poetry Capitalize all words except articles, conjunctions, and prepositions of less than five letters unless these occur in the first or last position in the title.

- *We Bombed in New Haven*
- *Reflections in a Golden Eye*
- "The Love Song of J. Alfred Prufrock"
- "The Lake Isle of Innisfree"
- *Two Against the Gods*

In titles that contain hyphenated words, capitalize if both parts of the hyphenated expression are nouns.

- *Confessions of an English Opium-Eater*
- *History of the English-speaking Peoples*

Titles of Persons Occupying High Office Capitalize the name of the office whether or not the holder of the office is named.

- The President of the United States, the Senator, the Secretary of State, the Prime Minister, the Secretary-General

CARELESSNESS

Like spelling errors, all errors caused by carelessness are inexcusable. They are the mark of lazy, immature writing—the kind of writing that bedevils teachers, editors, and critics. Ignorance of a grammatical or stylistic point is understandable; carelessness is not. Most of the careless errors that creep into papers should be caught before the final revision, and for that reason writers should complete their writing several days before the work is due and surely in plenty of time for a final retyping. Reviewing a paper several days after it has been written—just before final retyping—gives the writer a chance to view his work almost as a stranger will. He is thus more likely to catch errors.

CARET

The caret (∧) is the mark placed under or in a line of manuscript to indicate that something should be inserted at that point. The material to be inserted is written in the margin of a text that is to be submitted to a printer. In the case of student papers, the material to be inserted is more often inserted between the lines of the paper:

>   distinguished
> - He was one of the most ∧men I have ever known.

CASE

Case expresses the relationship between a noun or pronoun and another element in a sentence. The cases of nouns give little difficulty—there are only the common form and the possessive: boy, boys; boy's, boys'. The major trouble is with the case of pronouns after a linking verb. Informal English uses the objective (accusative) case, and formal English uses the subjective (nominative).

Formal   It is I.

Informal   It is me.

Another major problem with case is the confusion of *who* and *whom*:

Informal   the man *who* you were speaking to

Formal   the man to *whom* you were speaking

Correct   She is the one *who* can give you directions. (*She* can give you directions.)

Correct   Percy is the one *whom* many people regard with favor. (Many people regard *Percy* with favor.)

Correct   The actor *who* I thought would get the Oscar received only applause. (I thought *he* would get the Oscar.)

Incorrect   The company official *whom* I thought would be fired received a raise. (Would you say, I thought *him* would be fired?)

The object of a preposition is always in the objective case.

Correct   The college will offer scholarships to them.

[CA]

Correct   The contract is acceptable to him and me.

Incorrect   I shall give this to whomever applies for it. (The pronoun *whoever* should be substituted here. It is the subject of *applies*, not the object of *to*. The clause *whoever applies for it* is the object of *to*.)

In elliptical constructions using *than* or *as*, the case of a pronoun is established by the use of the pronoun.

Correct   We can operate the snow plow as well as *they*. (... as well as *they* can operate the snow plow.)

Correct   The dean stayed later than *I*. (... than *I* stayed.)

Correct   I like you better than *her*. (I like you better than I like *her*.)

CHILDISH STYLE

Childish style is writing filled characteristically with exclamation points, underscoring, ellipsis, and excessive use of outworn adjectives. It is a style of writing that tries to convey excitement and emphasis by punctuation rather than by effective writing.

CLARITY

Clarity is the essential quality of good prose style. In the process of trying to make yourself easily understood, you must pay special attention to sentence structure, diction, and logical presentation of ideas. Granted that certain ideas are inherently more difficult to understand than others, the writer still must strive to achieve clarity no matter what subject he is discussing. The college theme writer who uses the excuse that the profundity of his ideas explains his lack of clarity is not apt to reach sympathetic ears.

To guarantee clarity in writing, first ask yourself what you are trying to tell your reader. Can you express it in a single sentence? Almost any idea can be expressed in a single English sentence. Once you have established just what you want to say, what ideas and information must then be presented to develop your main idea? Determine the logical order of these elements and write an outline. From that point on, you have only to follow your outline, expressing yourself in straightforward sentences composed of the precise words needed to convey your thoughts.

CLAUSE

A clause is a group of words having a subject and predicate. An *independent clause* may stand alone as a sentence.

- She drank two cups of tea to be polite, but her husband refused to drink any. (Two independent clauses connected by a coordinating conjunction, *but*.)

A *subordinate clause* may not stand alone as a sentence. It must be joined to some other element in a sentence by a subordinating conjunction, real or implied.

- Several of the men *who* visited the campus were astonished at its rapid growth.
- The tree you cut down stood on the plaintiff's property. (The subordinating conjunction *that* is understood between *tree* and *you*. The dependent clause is *you cut down*.)

Clauses are classified according to the grammatical function performed—noun, adjective, adverb.

Noun-Subject   *Whoever pays the bill* calls the tune.
Noun-Object   He believed *that the time had come for action*.
Adjective   The man *who vaulted the fence* was being chased.
Adverb   He replied that he would go *when he was ready*.

COHERENCE

Coherence is the relationship between concepts. It may refer to the relationship between concepts in a sentence, between sentences, or between paragraphs. Lapses in coherence often occur because the writer inadvertently omits a vital link he does not wish to omit: he knows his subject so well that his mind skips ahead in the development. Effective outlines, complete down to the last item in the development of a main idea, can prevent such lapses. Careful revision, in which the writer acts as a disinterested reader of his own material, will also check this type of error.

When a writer has not thought through his argument before beginning to write, he should not be surprised to find that his discussion seems incoherent to his reader. Typically, he falls prey to such logical fallacies as the following: *post hoc ergo propter hoc,* in which causation is found between events merely because one occurs before the other; begging the question; arguing in a circle; and *non sequitur,* in which irrelevant reasons are put forward for holding a particular position.

COLLECTIVE NOUN

A collective noun is one that names a group of persons, objects, or acts. A collective noun may be treated as a singular or as a plural, depending on the sense in which it is intended. Once the choice has been made, the writer must stay with his decision.

> *Correct*   The majority of the group *is* for the proposal, and *it* insists on *its* right.
>
> *Correct*   The majority of the group *are* for the proposal, and *they* insist on *their* right.

The distinction between the two sentences is that the writer of the first sentence was thinking of the *majority* as a bloc, the writer of the second as many individuals. Consider the following pair of sentences, both correct:

- The team decided to walk off the field because *they* thought the umpire was being unfair to *them.*
- The team decided to walk off the field because *it* thought the umpire was being unfair to *it.*

A case can be made for both these constructions. You can decide which of the two you prefer. Just remember that the next time you deal with such nouns as *group, family, team, audience, orchestra, cast,* and *number,* you must decide whether you intend a plural or a singular and then stay with your choice.

COLLOQUIAL LANGUAGE

Colloquial language is the language we speak rather than the language we normally write. Informal English differs from formal English in that it is closer to colloquial usage. There is nothing wrong with the use of colloquial language, but the inappropriate use of colloquial language in general and formal writing presents problems. Thus, *ain't* is a handy and widespread locution that is acceptable in colloquial English, and unacceptable in general and formal written English. So-called slang and substandard English abound in rich expressions that have their place in communication, the only restriction being that, as writers, we must always choose the right place and the right time.

COLON

A colon (:) is used (1) to set off a series of words, phrases, or clauses from the rest of a sentence; (2) to restate, explain, or illustrate a statement immediately before it; (3) to introduce a quotation of more than five lines; (4) to introduce a quotation in a sentence when the quotation is not closely related to the sentence; (5) after the salutation in formal letters; (6) between hours and minutes when numerals are used; (7) between proportions in scientific expressions; (8) to replace a semicolon for stylistic purposes; and (9) in footnotes and bibliographies.

1. Series Use a colon to set off a series from the remainder of a sentence.

- Sean checked off the items he would need: hip boots, rod and reel, flies, and landing net.

2. Explanation Use a colon to introduce an explanation, restatement, or illustration of a preceding statement.

- Several persons recommended him for the job because of his background: five years at Georgia Tech, three years in the Army Engineers, and four years with the du Pont Company.
- After weighing all the evidence for several hours, the jury brought in the verdict: murder in the first degree.

3. Long Quotation   Use a colon to introduce a quotation of more than five printed lines.

> While Samuel Butler was justly famous as a novelist, he was also an early biological theorist:
>
>> Surely the theory that I have indicated above makes the reason plain why no organism can permanently outlive its experience of past lives. The death of a body such as the crayfish is due to the social condition becoming more complex than there is memory of past experience to deal with. Hence social disruption, insubordination, and decay. The crayfish dies as the state dies, and all states that we have heard of die sooner or later. There are some savages who have not yet arrived at the conception that all things die sooner or later.
>
> —*Unconscious Memory*, p. 148.

4. Quotation Within Sentence   Use a colon when incorporating a quotation into a sentence if it cannot be run in with a comma or without punctuation. The colon implies that the quotation is only loosely related to the sentence.

- In a preface to one of his lesser known works, he writes: "While a trifling success would much gratify, failure would not wholly discourage me from another effort."

5. Salutation   Use a colon after the salutation of a formal letter.

- Dear Professor:
- Dear Sirs:

6. Time   Use a colon between hours and minutes in giving time.

- 12:30, 1:45

7. Proportions   Use a colon in giving proportions.

- The fertilizer contained nitrogen and potash in the proportion of 5:10.

8. Stylistic Reasons   Use a colon, not a comma and conjunction, when you desire a more complete break between clauses.

- The citizen in any successful democracy should not only cast a vote: he should cast an educated vote.
- There was only one thing left for him to do: he tore off his shoes and leapt into the water.

9. Footnotes and Bibliography   Use a colon between the place of publication and the name of the publisher in footnotes and bibliographies, if you are following the older bibliographic practice. Note that, although this form of footnoting is not followed by the authors of this book, it is included here because some schools still adhere to this practice. (For the recommended form of footnotes, see FOOTNOTES.)

Footnote   Austin Clarke, *Flight to Africa* (Dublin: Dolmen Press, 1963), p. 21.

Bibliographic Entry   Clarke, Austin. *Flight to Africa.* Dublin: Dolmen Press, 1963.

COMMA

The comma is the most common mark of punctuation and the most commonly misused. Partial blame for this misuse must rest with those teachers of composition who lose patience with pupils struggling to learn the intricacies of the uses of the comma. After all, punctuation is "unnatural." (Can you blame the young who desperately insert a comma in a sentence whenever they pause in their writing? And can you blame those who say, "I use a comma whenever I would pause if I were reading a sentence aloud"? This might work if we all breathed evenly.) The rationale for the comma, as for all marks of punctuation, is that we can help our readers understand us more readily with consistent punctuation than without it.

The main uses of the comma are: (1) to separate coordinate clauses; (2) to set off nonrestrictive clauses and phrases; (3) to set off introductory elements; (4) to set off parenthetic expressions; (5) to separate the elements of a series; (6) to separate coordinate adjectives;

and (7) to set off miscellaneous expressions, such as dates, geographic entities, and units of counting.

1. Coordinate Clauses   Use a comma and a coordinating conjunction between coordinate clauses.

- The suspect entered the building, and the detective followed closely behind.
- Relative frequency of occurrence is important, but it is not the only factor to consider.
- Will was impatient to get to the soccer field, for the match was scheduled for two o'clock.

If you cannot see that this use of the comma is important, consider the role it plays in each of the next examples:

- The wolf devoured the dying hare, and the dog ran away.
- The tree lost all its leaves, and the hedge was not far behind.
- The firemen played their hoses on the raging fire, and the policemen kept the crowds back.

If there were no comma, the reader might think that the wolf devoured the dog, the tree lost the hedge, and the firemen soaked the policemen. The comma between coordinate clauses prevents even a moment's uncertainty.

2. Nonrestrictive Modifiers   Use a pair of commas to separate nonrestrictive phrases and clauses from the rest of a sentence. If the phrase or clause introduces or terminates the sentence, use only one comma.

- Charles Dickens, *one of the most noted of English novelists,* was attracted to the deformed, half-witted, and abandoned.
- Dublin, *which has some of the most noted Georgian buildings in Europe,* is now strongly under the influence of modern architectural styles.
- Many consider the modern era in Mexico to have begun with the Mexican Revolution, *surely one example of a good use of force.*
- *A man endowed with the virtue of humility,* President

28   [CO]

Coolidge avoided intervention and sent an emissary bent on a peaceful solution.

3. **Introductory Elements** Use a comma to separate all clauses, verbal phrases, and prepositional phrases of more than three words that precede the main statement of a sentence.

- Since his original premises seemed now to be open to doubt, he laid aside the line of investigation and thought out the problem once more.
- Showing modesty, most successful men deprecate their own achievements.
- With hardly a trace of emotion, Inspector O'Byrne continued his inspection of the scene of the crash.
- In order that men may live rather than merely exist, they must have a reasonable income.

4. **Parenthetic Expressions** Use a comma to separate parenthetic expressions from the rest of a sentence.

- The workers must, of course, have adequate leisure.
- Adequate leisure, to be sure, means time to pursue interests other than those connected with work.

5. **Lists and Series** Use a comma between elements in a series or list. However, if the elements of the series are internally punctuated, use a semicolon.

- She selected three pins, two ties, a sweater, and a brooch.
- They marched before the retiring Mayor in regular order: the Police Band first, then the Fire Band, and finally the Sanitation Fife and Drum Corps.
- He ordered cereal, which turned out to be indigestible; two slices of toast, neither of which had been near a toaster that day; and ham and eggs, which bore little resemblance to what he remembered of such foods in his mother's kitchen.

Some writers insist on omitting the comma normally preceding the *and* before the final element in a series. Yet there is no adequate justification for this practice. Inserting this comma, which may not appear necessary much of the time, may occasionally prevent serious misunderstanding.

6. Coordinate Adjectives Use commas to separate two or more adjectives in a series if they modify a noun in the same manner.

- A *thick, solid* door stood under a deeply curved arch.

Thick and *solid* both modify *door* in the same manner, so they are called *coordinate adjectives.* Notice that the word *and* can stand in place of the comma between the adjectives *thick* and *solid.*

- The *hot, sticky, humid* air made everyone miserable.

Again, all three adjectives modify the noun in the same manner. The word *and* could again be used in place of the commas: hot *and* sticky *and* humid air. Wherever *and* can be used between adjectives, a comma is called for.

- An old oaken bucket lay beside the abandoned well.

Old modifies *oaken bucket*; *old* is not coordinate with *oaken.* You would not say *old and oaken bucket;* therefore, no comma can be inserted.

7. Miscellaneous Uses Use a comma between the day of the month and the year; after the salutation in a personal letter; between city or county, and state; in figures, to separate thousands, millions, etc.; with names in direct address; and after exclamations.

- June 29, 1971; March 11, 1984 (Usage tends to omit the comma between the month and the year: December 1975.)
- Dear Joan,
- Wilmington, Ohio; Suffern, Rockland County, New York
- 25,480   1,399,467   221,000,000
- John, I want to tell you a story.
- Gosh, that was a good game. Oh, what a beautiful morning!

COMMA FAULT

Comma fault is the name given by teachers of composition to the failure to insert the proper connective between two or more independent clauses. Comma faults are of two types: the use of a comma to join two independent clauses that really do not belong together, and the use of a comma between independent clauses when some other connective is needed. The writer whose sentence has been labeled *comma fault* must look for the connection between clauses and decide whether he needs a semicolon, a conjunction, or a period. Examine the following examples of comma faults and their revisions:

Comma Fault   The Hemingway hero is a mystery, how did he start, where did he come from?

Revised   The Hemingway hero is a mystery. How did he start, and where did he come from?

Revised   How did the mystery of the Hemingway hero originate?

Comma Fault   Four volumes of the work have been set in type, the first will be issued within two months.

Revised   Four volumes of the work have been set in type; the first will be issued within two months.

Comma Fault   I believed that his advice was sound, nevertheless I acted on it with caution.

Revised   I believed that his advice was sound; nevertheless, I acted on it with caution.

Comma Fault   All nations seeking to industrialize should look at their educational systems, they would soon realize that industry needs many technicians.

Revised   All nations seeking to industrialize should look at their education systems, for they would soon realize that industry needs many technicians.

Run-together sentences of the types shown are common in the writing of the young, but by the time a student reaches college, he should have overcome this fault. If you are prone to this error, carefully reread every sentence you write to see whether it is indeed a valid sentence.

COMPARE, CONTRAST

When *compare* is used to point out similarities, *to* is used with it. When *compare* is used in the sense of "examine" (point out similarities and differences), *with* is used.

- Shall I compare thee to a summer's day? (Shakespeare had in mind the similarities between them.)
- He compared the errors in my paper to the errors in Kate's paper. (The teacher said they were similar.)
- He compared Yeats's poetry with Blake's. (He showed how the poetry was similar and different.)

Contrast points out differences and is normally followed by *with*.

- The book contrasts the foreign policy of the Soviet Union with that of India.

COMPARISON OF MODIFIERS

Adjectives and adverbs have comparative and superlative forms in addition to absolute forms. The comparative indicates differences in degree between two elements.

- John is taller than Harry.
- It is often difficult to determine which city has the larger population, Tokyo or New York.

The superlative indicates the difference in degree among three or more elements.

- It is often difficult to determine which city has the largest population, New York, Tokyo, or London.

In colloquial language, the superlative is often used when no specific comparison is intended.

- He is the greatest.
- You are the smoothest.

With adjectives and adverbs of three or more syllables, the comparative and superlative are generally expressed by using *more* and *most* with the absolute form.

| beautiful | more beautiful | most beautiful |
| immediate | more immediate | most immediate |

Many adjectives and adverbs can be compared either by adding *er* and *est* to the absolute or by using *more* and *most*.

often	more often	most often
often	oftener	oftenest
kind	more kind	most kind
kind	kinder	kindest

The *er, est* form stresses the quality, *more* and *most* the degree of difference.

COMPLEMENT

Complement is the name given an adjective or noun that follows a linking verb. The name is derived from a Latin word meaning *that which fills up*, and "fill up" is what a complement does for an otherwise meaningless linking verb. After all, we cannot *is, are,* or *be* unless we *is, are,* or *be* something!

- He was *handsome* in his youth.
- Dr. Murray was the *surgeon* in the case.
- The dish tastes *delicious.*
- As usual, the sophomores sounded *ridiculous.*

COMPOUND PREDICATE

A compound predicate consists of two or more verbs having the same subject. Two compound verbs are not punctuated; three or more are punctuated as a series.

- The wind *lashed* the cliffs and *leveled* the trees.
- The wind *lashed* the cliffs, *leveled* the trees, and *tore* at the homes along the ridge.

Compound predicates tighten up the structure of a sentence, preventing overly simple, or primer, sentences.

- The wind lashed the cliffs. It leveled the trees. It tore at the homes along the ridge.

COMPOUND SENTENCE

A compound sentence consists of two or more independent clauses. The principal difficulty with compound sentences is punctuation. A compound sentence may be punctuated with a comma followed by a coordinating conjunction, or by a semicolon, either alone or followed by a conjunctive adverb.

Coordinating Conjunctions—and, or, for, but, yet, nor, while— *Preceded by a Comma*

- He was certain that he had left the keys in the house, *but* he could not find them.
- The spectators roared their approval, *and* the players continued to punch one another clumsily.
- Several centuries have elapsed since man is supposed to have come out of the Dark Ages, *yet* we do not seem to be any more tolerant of our fellow men than were our earliest ancestors.

The Semicolon, with or without a Conjunctive Adverb— nevertheless, however, moreover, accordingly, furthermore, indeed—*in Compound Sentences*

- My schoolmates talked of the incident incessantly instead of paying attention to their courses; they talked of little else until the end of the term.
- It was Nature's fashion; she never quite reacts as we expect her to.
- She relied exclusively on the darker tones in painting portraits; *moreover,* her subjects approved her work.
- The ambition of the Romans was confined to the land; *nevertheless,* Augustus stationed two permanent fleets in the most convenient ports of Italy.
- But such was not the case; *indeed,* it has been claimed that such transoceanic voyages are impossible.

COMPOUND SUBJECT

When a verb has more than one subject, the subject is compound. The verb following a compound subject is plural unless both parts of the compound subject refer to the same thing.

- The ball and the bat *are* part of the Babe Ruth Collection.
- Truth and courage *are* no longer found in some parts of our society unless the investigator is willing to search hard.
- Chicago and its environs *is* in the midst of the usual summer heat wave.
- That the team had won and that it had won decisively *was* of no importance to him.

CONCRETE WORDS

Concrete words name things that can be seen and touched—head, hair, hedge, window, gas station, garage. Concrete words are always preferable to abstract words, which designate acts, theories, ideas, qualities, relationships. Of course, one cannot use concrete words exclusively to describe the abstract. The mistake poor writers make is to use abstract words when the situation calls for the concrete. The result is sentences cluttered with words that may appear high-sounding, but actually are at least one step removed from telling a clear story.

CONDITIONAL CLAUSE

A conditional clause states the action or condition necessary for the validity of the main statement of a sentence. The most common conjunction used with conditional clauses is *if*, but *if not, unless,* and *whether* are also used. Conditions may be classified as *practical* or as *contrary to fact*. This classification determines the mood of the verb in the conditional clause.

Practical conditions are those in which the main statement will be possible if the conditional statement is fulfilled.

- If you *see* the signal, call out.

- If the ship *does* not *arrive* on time, we will lose our hotel reservations.
- Unless we *honor* this important commitment, the Secretary said, our allies will not believe any of our other professions of commitment.

For practical conditions, use the simpler form of the verb in the conditional statement, the simple or future form in the main statement.

Conditions contrary to fact are those in which the statement in the conditional clause is obviously not true and cannot become true. In formal expression, use the subjunctive mood in the conditional clause, the simple or future form in the main statement.

- If I *were* you, I would walk on the other side of the road.
- If he *be* the man he claims to be, he will not press for payment under these circumstances.
- If we really *were* sincere, we would not behave in that way.

This use of the subjunctive mood in conditions contrary to fact is dying out even in formal English, but it is still useful to express fine shades of meaning. Consider the following pair of sentences:

- If he *be* the man he claims to be, he will not press for payment under these circumstances.
- If he *is* the man he claims to be, he will not press for payment under these circumstances.

In the first sentence, there is no doubt that he is *not* the man he claims to be. In the second sentence, the poor wretch is given a chance of showing that he *is* the man he claims to be. Again, when a man says, "If I *am* elected, I will not serve," he means that he may be elected and that he will not serve. But when a man says, "If I *were* elected, I would not serve," he means that his chance of being elected is nonexistent. He gives up nothing by making this bold statement.

All this adds up to one consideration: concern yourself with the problem of the correct form of the verb in a conditional clause when you are on your best behavior. When you are concerned with subtleties of expression, use the subjunctive mood for conditions contrary to fact. This means using *were* in place of *was* in the first and third persons singular.

- If I *were* king....
- If he *were* the last man on earth....

CONJUNCTION

A conjunction is a word that joins words, phrases, or clauses. *Coordinating* conjunctions join clauses of equal weight, independent clauses. *Subordinating* conjunctions introduce statements that describe or qualify a word or concept in the main clause.

The accurate use of conjunctions is one sign of a mature writer, and care should be taken both in formal and informal writing that the most accurate conjunction is used. When we speak with another person, we can indicate a great deal concerning the relationships between concepts by the tone of our speech, by pauses, shrugs, and facial expressions. In writing we are deprived of these valuable tools, and a great deal of the burden of expressing our thoughts precisely must be carried by our conjunctions. The following sentences demonstrate the importance of conjunctions:

- The war will end when we stop bombing.
- The war will end if we stop bombing.
- The war will end whenever we stop bombing.
- The war will end although we stop bombing.
- The war will end after we stop bombing.
- The war will end because we stop bombing.

CONJUNCTIVE ADVERB

Conjunctive adverbs are adverbs that can be used as conjunctions between independent clauses: *accordingly, consequently, furthermore, however, moreover, nevertheless, therefore, thus.* Such words can convey a good deal of information, so we must not be afraid of them. Yet they carry a penalty. Conjunctive adverbs require a semicolon before and a comma after them. For this reason we use them only when necessary, as a rule only in formal writing. Poor writers tend to rely heavily on these words, and their writing becomes ponderous. Many engineering and scientific journals are prime examples of excessive reliance on these conjunctions.

[CO]

Consider the following pair of sentences, both of which are correct:

- An editor can improve a manuscript, *but* he cannot put in it what is not there.
- An editor can improve a manuscript; *however*, he cannot put in it what is not there.

The choice you make between these sentences is based not on any question of grammatical correctness, but on style. The same choice is possible in the next pair of sentences:

- The Senator tried his best to push the bill through, *yet* he was not able to get it out of committee.
- The Senator tried his best to push the bill through; *nevertheless*, he was not able to get it out of committee.

The next time you write a paper—particularly an expository theme—check through your sentences to see how many conjunctive adverbs you have used. Have you *thussed, howevered,* and *therefored* your reader into a state of disbelief or revulsion?

CONTACT CLAUSE

Contact clauses are two or more coordinate clauses that stand together with a comma between them. Such clauses are more characteristic of narrative than of expository writing, but when used *consciously* as a stylistic device, they are appropriate in formal as well as informal writing. For student and beginning writers, what appears to be a pair of contact clauses frequently turns out to be a comma fault. The distinction between contact clauses and a comma fault is difficult to determine, so most teachers and many editors are inclined to regard the omission of a coordinating conjunction between clauses as poor style. There is no rule that tells when and when not to use contact clauses. One bit of good advice is never to use them in a freshman composition course. A more serious suggestion is to use contact clauses when the clauses are brief and closely related in meaning.

- Speak up, you will probably be right.
- Eat little, live long.

CONTRACTION

Contractions are words from which unstressed syllables have been omitted—*won't, isn't*. Since they are common in conversation, most dialogue uses contractions. They are also used in informal and general English, but not in formal English. Consider the audience for whom you are writing when you are considering whether to use a contraction.

COORDINATING CONJUNCTION

A coordinating conjunction is used to join two or more independent clauses. The principal coordinating conjunctions are *and, but, for, nor, or, while, yet,* and *so*. When a coordinating conjunction is used, it is preceded by a comma.

- The month of November drew slowly to a close, and the boys were satisfied with the continuing mild weather.
- Many of these students could not write even simple sentences, but the instructors determined to do what they could for them.

Compound constructions, such as compound subjects and compound predicates, should not be punctuated unless they are exceptionally long or complicated.

- The theater *was closed* and completely *redecorated* once the season was over.
- Despite all our efforts, there was nothing *to do* but *to abandon* the search.
- Professor Schmidt *reviewed* the academic background and scholarly accomplishments of all the candidates for the position, and *agreed* that only two of them were worthy of further consideration.
- The aerodynamic design was *noteworthy* in several respects but *deficient* in others, and so was returned to the design team for further refinement.

CORRELATIVE CONJUNCTION

Correlative conjunctions are used in pairs with grammatically similar constructions. Although purists insist that both such constructions be

[CO]

exactly parallel, some shifts are common—particularly in informal writing. The principal correlative conjunctions are *either . . . or, not only . . . but also, neither . . . nor,* and *whether . . . or.*

- *Either* you go *or* I go.
- *Not only* was she a good student, *but* she was *also* well liked by her classmates.
- *Neither* you *nor* your friend may stay late.
- *Whether* she walks *or* runs, she is always in a hurry.

D

DANGLING MODIFIER

A dangling modifier is one that appears to modify a word it cannot reasonably relate to—the modifier has been misplaced. When you discover such an error of style, you must usually recast the entire sentence to place the modifier as close as possible to the word or construction it modifies, or you must supply a word or construction that can be modified properly.

Incorrect Dashing through the room at full speed, the door obstructed him. (The door cannot dash through a room.)

Correct As he dashed through the room, the door obstructed his exit.

Incorrect To wield it properly, the handle must be grasped. (We have no idea what *it* is. The previous sentence may have given the explanation, or it may not have. At any rate, in this sentence, it looks as though we want to wield a handle. Surely there must be more than that.)

Correct To wield the axe properly, the handle must be grasped.

Correct To wield the axe properly, one must grasp the handle.

Incorrect He was arraigned for filching fish in Felony Court. (Did he filch the fish in Court, or some other place? Surely he must have been arraigned in Court.)

Correct He was arraigned in Felony Court for filching fish.

In most cases, dangling modifiers do not confuse the reader. Relying on context clues, he is well aware that a young man is dashing through the room, that it is an axe that must be wielded, and that the fish-filching did not occur in Felony Court. Yet the writer must beware. Is there any chance that confusion can result from a dangling construction? If there is, the construction must be avoided. Is extra effort needed to understand what a writer is saying? Reading is difficult enough without making it unnecessarily difficult. Is there any chance that a construction can be interpreted in such a way that the writer is held up to ridicule? Careful editing can prevent such constructions.

DASH

The dash is used (1) to indicate a sharp turn in thought, (2) to indicate that a summary statement follows, and (3) to enclose parenthetic statements when the author wishes to give them more stress than they would have if they were enclosed by commas.

1. Shift in Thought

- He was motivated by a love for power—not freedom—and he acquired as much power as he dared.

- The general effect of the book—to call it by a more exalted name than it deserves—is to pitch readers into fits of laughter.

2. Summary Statement

- He is all that constitutes a gentleman—in carriage, gait, address, gesture, voice, courtesy, and self-assurance.

- The ride to the airport, the wait as baggage and tickets were checked, the last farewells—all that was over, and they were off.

3. Parenthetic Statement

- Many subjects—zoology and anthropology, for example—interested him enough to make him want to remain on campus for another year.

- The polished manners and elegance of dress—acquired in society—are by society admired.

Many writers are frightened by the dash because they are uncertain of its proper use and its appropriateness in general writing. The dash should be thought of as a mark that emphasizes sentence elements that do not occupy emphatic positions. If used sparingly for that purpose, the dash is effective. To use the dash the way teenagers do in their letters to friends—as the only mark of punctuation—is to rob it of its ability to heighten and clarify.

DEADWOOD

Deadwood is the term used by teachers and editors to describe writing that is too full of meaningless words, phrases, and sentences. Deadwood calls for unrelenting use of the red pencil in every revision, striking out anything that does not contribute to meaning. In the deadwood forests of much student writing, the most prominent specimens are strings of adjectives that could be eliminated if the proper noun were used. Another rich harvest would be possible if we examined every sentence within a paragraph to see whether there is sufficient duplication to enable us to eliminate entire sentences. In dealing with the problem, ask yourself what each sentence really says and whether the meaning is (1) different from what the rest of the paragraph says and (2) useful in the development of the paragraph. If sentences do not meet these two tests, strike them out.

DECLENSION

Declension is the inflection of nouns and pronouns to show gender, number, and case. English has no declension in the sense that Latin, German, and Greek have; the noun has only two forms to show differences in function (case)—the common form and the possessive. Pronouns have three cases—subjective, objective, and possessive—but the declension is not regular. The lack of declension is one indication of the maturity of the English language as well as an explanation of why the grammar of English is so difficult for native and foreign students alike.

DELETE

"Delete" is an expression used by teachers and editors to signify that they are displeased with the quality of the writing before them. They abbreviate delete as *dele*, as the Greek lower case delta (δ), or as a line drawn through the offending material. The frequent use of *dele* in your papers should alert you to the need for more rigorous editing on your part before submitting future papers.

DEMONSTRATIVES

Demonstratives are adjectives and pronouns that point to other words.

- *This* hat looks as good to me *this* year as it did last year.
- *Those* cadets never seem to tire of parading back and forth.
- *This* is the best book I have read so far.
- *These* are the things some of us love, if we are to believe the songwriter.

DICTION

Diction refers to the words we use in speaking and writing. The term is used by teachers to call attention to faulty use of words, which can cause the reader to misunderstand or inadequately appreciate the intent of the writer. It goes without saying that words must be chosen precisely if we are to write well. A student writer who is inaccurate in his choice of words must become a devotee of the dictionary and thesaurus. This practice, combined with a systematic program of vocabulary enrichment, will usually cure problems of diction. But this is not to say that the best words are rare and elegant. Everyday words can effectively describe most of our thoughts. The problem is one of choosing the right word, not the fanciest.

DIVISION OF WORDS

There are widely accepted rules governing the division of words in a manuscript, but most publishers and teachers prefer a jagged right-hand margin with few, if any, divided words to one that is even but full of divided words. This relieves the printer or the teacher of the job of wondering whether the writer intends a hyphenated word or a divided word.

Some general rules for dividing words are helpful. (1) Never divide a word when only one letter will be left on a line. (2) It is always permissible to divide between double consonants. (3) Both divided parts should be pronounceable. (4) Words of one syllable are never divided.

DOUBLING FINAL CONSONANTS

The most useful spelling rule in English concerns the doubling of final consonants before adding suffixes. This rule is without exception, which is why it is so useful. Although it may appear complicated, it is worth learning.

One Syllable Words In words of one syllable ending in a single consonant preceded by a single vowel, double the final consonant before adding a suffix beginning with a vowel.

- bat: batted, batting, batty
- sin: sinner, sinning (but sinful)
- run: runner, running, runny

Words of More Than One Syllable In words of more than one syllable ending in a single consonant preceded by a single vowel, double the final consonant before adding a suffix beginning with a vowel *if* the accent in the original word is on the final syllable and adding the suffix does not cause the accent to shift.

- refer: referred, referring (but referee, reference)
- confer: conferred, conferring (but conferee, conference)

Words ending in a double consonant retain the double consonant when followed by a suffix beginning with a vowel, but usually lose a consonant when followed by a suffix beginning with a consonant.

- will: willed, willing (wilful *also* willful)
- skill: skilled (skilful *also* skillful)

Modern American usage would prefer the single consonant for *wilful* and *skilful*.

Wherever you encounter an apparent exception to any parts of the rule stated for doubling final consonants, check first to see whether all parts of the rule obtain. *Transferable* is not an exception, because the accent has shifted from the *fer* syllable to the *trans* syllable; *excellent* is not an exception because the accent has shifted; and so it goes. Learn this spelling rule.

DUE TO

Opinion is divided and vocal on the propriety of using the prepositional phrase *due to*. Purists insist that *due*, originally an adjective, should not be used in a prepositional phrase. They insist that *owing to* or *because of* should be substituted. According to recent studies, however, *due to* is used in over half the situations in which any of the three expressions could have occurred. It seems unlikely that this trend can be stopped by the opposition of teachers, editors, and writers of books on style. We might point out that *due to* does not appear to be as resolute as *because of* or *owing to* and that *due to* looks as though it may be more at home in bank statements than in English sentences.

E

EACH

Although *each* is singular, it carries the concept of plurality (*each of them*). This concept of plurality causes problems in the reference of pronouns and the number of verbs.

> *Formal*   *Each* of the performers carried out *his* task perfectly.
>
> *Informal*   *Each* of the performers carried out *their* tasks perfectly.
>
> *Formal*   *Each* of these problems *is* an aspect of a larger problem.

Remember that most of the papers you will write in college are formal papers, so take care not to be lulled into carelessness by the apparent anarchy of current popular practice. Stay on the safe side.

ED

Teachers are constantly marking papers with dropped *eds*, and many an editor has inserted his share of *eds* in copy prepared for publication. The problem arises partly because many past forms ending in *d* tend to drop the *d* when followed by a word beginning with *t*, as in *iced tea*. Words ending in *d* before *t* often have both sounds assimilated into one: in regard to, in regar tə; in respect to, in respec tə. While this practice is suitable for some speech, it is not acceptable in writing. The past tense and the past participle of regular verbs end in *ed*. Only in dialogue can these letters be omitted. (ə is defined under SCHWA.)

In cases of nouns that can function as adjectives, locutions have arisen in which the omission of *ed* is accepted: ice cream for iced cream, whip cream for whipped cream, frame house for framed house, post free for posted free, pickle relish for pickled relish, one hundred room mansion for one hundred roomed mansion, patch quilt for patched quilt.

EI, IE

The old rule—now practically as well known as the Pledge of Allegiance—has it that "*i* comes before *e* except after *c*." Instead of going on to repeat all the words that are exceptions to this rule, learn to add, "but *e* after *i* when the sound is $\bar{a}$."

- achieve, believe, friend; deign, eight, weight

But there are the exceptions: *seize, weir, weird.* Remember them.

EITHER

Used as a pronoun, *either* is singular. When acting as the antecedent of another pronoun, *either* is also treated as singular.

- Either *is* all right.
- Either the tractor or the car *is* always in need of repair.
- Either of the students *is* qualified for graduate school.
- Either of the students is able to explain *his* position on the matter satisfactorily.
- Either of the newspapers is going to have to redefine *its* position if *it* wants to retain respect.

ELLIPSIS

Ellipsis (... or ....) indicates that some material has been omitted from a quotation. Three periods indicates that the omitted material does not include the end of a sentence. Four periods indicates that the omitted material is from the end of a sentence or that more than one sentence has been omitted.

> They are ... dramas of thought, not of action.... He makes the character under dissection explain itself. In some cases deliberately, and in others consciously, it reveals its very inmost soul....
>
> —Ester Defries, *A Browning Primer*

Three periods can also be used in dialogue to indicate a pause in speech, but this mark is rare in student papers. Above all, do not use periods in numbers greater than four, and never use them to imply anything unstated. The so-called pregnant pause should be left to the correspondence of young lovers.

EMPHASIS

One way to give emphasis to your most important thoughts in writing is to assign them positions that naturally endow words with emphasis. Generally, the two most emphatic positions in a paper, paragraph, or sentence are the beginning and the end. In a paper, this means that the subject should be introduced in the opening of the paper and repeated in the closing. In a paragraph, the topic sentence should come first or last, depending on the paragraph structure desired. In a sentence, the subject and verb are the most emphatic elements and should occur close to the beginning of most sentences.

Emphasis can also be achieved by using clear and precise language and avoiding unnecessary words, which usually rob a thought of emphasis. Yet this does not mean that words can never be repeated or that thoughts can never be repeated. (Notice the repetition of *can never be repeated.*) Deliberate repetition adds emphasis, and even beginning writers can use this device effectively to make certain the reader grasps the message. But this repetition is never done well if it is done carelessly. When repetition results from carelessness, the trivial is repeated as often as the important.

EUPHEMISM

A euphemism is an expression used in place of a stronger expression that is generally unacceptable in formal English or considered offensive. Thus, writers have often substituted "woman of easy virtue" or "woman of ill repute" for *prostitute,* and Eugene O'Neill has one of his characters in *Ah, Wilderness!* say "whited sepulchre" when he means *prostitute.* O'Neill's expression is entirely in keeping with the social scene described in the play. Fortunately, under the pressure of modern writers, euphemisms are disappearing, yet they persist in much formal and general writing. Will we ever get over the expression "social disease" as a substitution for *venereal disease,* which is itself a euphemism for more specific ills of mankind?

EXCLAMATION POINT

The exclamation point is used after a forceful interjection or after a phrase, clause, or sentence that is exclamatory. Use the exclamation point sparingly. Excessive use is like crying wolf too often. And never—*repeat never*—use more than one exclamation point at a time.

EXPOSITORY WRITING

Expository writing is writing that is intended primarily to inform. This characteristic sets limits on the nature of paragraph development and on the choice of language and stylistic constructions. Almost all writing in college, except for creative writing, is expository.

F

FARTHER, FURTHER

No distinction is made between *farther* and *further* in general writing, but in formal writing *farther* refers to distance, *further* to abstract concepts.

- The village is twenty miles *farther* downstream than my map indicates.
- If you go any *further* with this kind of behavior, Tim, you will soon be in trouble with the authorities.

In general writing, *further* would be used in both sentences.

FIGURATIVE LANGUAGE

Language can be literal or figurative. When it is figurative, we borrow terms that are literal in one context and use them in another, where they become figurative. Thus we can say that a baseball batter has swung his bat and hit the ball. That is literally what has happened. But the sports writer, desperate at having to describe the same action again and again for six months, might write:

- The batter cut at a jug-handle curve and rocketed it into the grandstand.

This writing relies for its descriptive power on figurative language. After all, the batter does not intend to *cut* the ball literally, nor does the curve have a *jug handle*—only jugs have. And a *rocket* is surely nowhere in sight.
  Figurative language is appropriate when it is fresh and adds force and character to writing. It is inappropriate when it is stale, worn out, hackneyed. Needless to say, most attempts at figurative language by mediocre sports writers end in disaster. What may once have been a sparkling metaphor in the hands of the exceptional writer ends too

often as a cliche. In your own writing, avoid any figure of speech you have heard or read. Be original.

FINITE VERB

A finite verb is limited in person (first, second, or third), number (singular or plural), or tense (present, past, or future). Verb forms that are not so limited are *infinite:* the infinitive (to run, to have run) and the participle (running, run).

FOOTNOTES & BIBLIOGRAPHY

Whenever a writer uses material from a published source—whether quoting directly or paraphrasing—that use must be noted in both footnote and bibliographic entries. For a footnote use the author's full name, title of the work, place and date of publication, and the page number:

- [1] Compton Mackenzie, *Carnival* (London, 1912), p. 159.
- [2] C. S. Lewis, "On Obstinacy in Belief," *Sewanee Review,* LXIII (Autumn, 1955), p. 527.

In the text the footnote number should be placed at the end of the material quoted and above the line, thus.[3]

The bibliography is an alphabetical list of the works cited in the footnotes, with the author's last name first:

- Lewis, C. S. "On Obstinacy in Belief," *Sewanee Review,* LXIII (Autumn, 1955), 525-538.
- Mackenzie, Compton, *Carnival.* London 1912.

FOR

For is both a conjunction and a preposition. When it is used as a conjunction, it is preceded by a comma.

- Evelyn was eager to go, for the dance was dreary and the hall cold and dark.

When *for* is used as a preposition, it usually is not preceded by a comma, but each case must be judged individually. When in doubt, check the rules for the use of the comma.

FOREIGN WORDS IN ENGLISH

The use of foreign words in English is a characteristic of the development of the English language. Most of these words have been assimilated—they no longer seem foreign. Words such as chauffeur, chassis, chivalry, honor, garage, kimono, and shibboleth have been accepted as English. There are, however, other words that are current but have not been assimilated: *faux pas, tête-à-tête, raison d'être,* etc. Some inexpert writers think that a slight sprinkling of foreign words in a paper or article is a mark of good style. It is not. Foreign words should not be used where there is a good English equivalent: there is no reason for writing *faux pas* when *mistake* will do. When a foreign word must be used (when there is no English equivalent), the word is underscored (italicized) in formal writing, but practice is divided in general writing. Consult a dictionary when in doubt.

Foreign-language words that have not been assimilated retain their accents, as in the examples above. Words borrowed from German are capitalized if they are nouns, since that is the practice in German: *Weltanschauung, Lebensraum.*

FORMAL ENGLISH

Formal English is the level of expression appropriate to formal writing and speech. When we mix words from one level of usage—formal, general, colloquial—with another, we may end up with expressions that are not satisfactory. It is true, however, that many words are appropriate to all levels of usage.

Consider this sentence, in which words from formal English seem out of place because most of the sentence is cast in general language:

- To an extraordinary degree, Hemingway and what he has written exist in a *synergetic* relationship, reinforcing and fulfilling each other; he has a personal legend that serves as an *ambiance* in which we read his work.

The student who wrote this ugly sentence has obviously taken from the work of a critic a few words that appealed to his undeveloped sense of style and has incorporated them in his own work.

FRAGMENTARY SENTENCE

A fragmentary sentence is one that lacks a subject or a verb or does not express a complete thought. Many good modern writers deliberately use fragments with great effect. But, as with so many aspects of style, the beginning writer is counseled properly to avoid fragments. In college papers, most fragmentary sentences are the result of carelessness. They add nothing to the development of a thought, but add to the discomfort of teacher and critic.

The most frequently encountered fragments are subordinate clauses or phrases treated as complete sentences; in most cases they should be joined to the preceding sentence.

Fragment   He walked for three hours in the hot sun. Because his car had run out of gas.

Sentence   He walked for three hours in the hot sun after his car had run out of gas.

Fragment   He was anxious about the interview. Apparently not being certain of his qualifications.

Sentence   Because he was uncertain of his qualifications, he was anxious about the interview.

Just because good modern writers employ the fragment occasionally, do not feel that you will suddenly reach a point in your development as a writer when your teachers will invite you to a polite tea and announce that from that day forward you will be entitled to use fragments whenever you want. The fact is that some writers do not use fragments at all and apparently survive.

G

GENDER

There are three genders in English: masculine, feminine, and neuter. Fortunately, we do not have to concern ourselves much with gender. The Romance languages, among others, are loaded with problems of gender that plague the unwary student.

Gender in English is indicated for most words by the use of pronouns (his, hers, its) or by the use of certain suffixes (authoress, hostess, aviatrix). Such feminine endings are eschewed by many female practitioners (imagine a women's liberationist-writer referring to herself as an authoress!) and will probably disappear from the language before too long. It is unlikely, however, that we will ever lose such useful terms as goose and gander, fox and vixen, bull and cow, rooster and hen, and lord and lady.

Most inanimate objects are referred to in the neuter, but ships and the moon remain feminine.

GENITIVE CASE

The genitive (possessive) case is the form of nouns and pronouns that shows possession. There are four ways to show possession in English:

1. The most common is the addition of an apostrophe and an *s* to a singular and some plural nouns.

- girl's book, men's clothing, King's Inn, woman's cloak, one hour's delay

Words ending in *s* take the apostrophe alone or apostrophe *s* if the combination is not displeasing,

- Yeats's plays, Euripides' plays

Plural nouns ending in *s* take the apostrophe alone.

- boys' clothing, nuns' habits, three weeks' holiday

[GE] 55

2. Possession can also be shown by using the *of* construction.

- the valley of the Boyne, the plays of Arthur Miller

3. The personal pronoun can be inflected to show possession:

- my book, our book, your book, his book, her book, its paws, their books

4. Possession can be indicated by a double genitive, combining the *of* construction with the possessive form. This form is often used to avoid ambiguity.

- *that picture of Eileen's* (The meaning is clear that we are referring to a picture *by* Eileen rather than *of* her. To say *Eileen's picture* may imply a portrait of Eileen or a picture drawn by her. The double genitive avoids this ambiguity.)

GERUND

A gerund is a verbal. It looks like a present participle, in that it is the *ing* form of the verb, but it functions as a *noun*, while the present participle functions as an *adjective*.

Gerund   *Fishing* was his favorite sport. (*Fishing* is the subject of the verb.)

Present Participle   *Fishing* up and down the river, he was a sight to behold. (*Fishing* is the modifier of *he*.)

As a verbal, a gerund may be modified by an adjective or an adverb, may take an object, and can perform any noun function.

- *Fishing* continually for salmon was his only pleasure.
- He enjoyed *entertaining*.
- *Entertaining* his guests afforded him pleasure.
- By *satisfying* his clients, he improved his prospects.
- Light *entertaining* is common in America.

The gerund, like the infinitive, can indicate voice and tense.

Active   *Seeing* popular places is his pastime. (present)

Passive   *Being seen* in popular places pleases some people. (present)

Active   *Having read* the book was achievement enough, he explained. (past)

Passive   *Having been seen* was what disturbed him most of all. (past)

Subject of the Gerund   A gerund may take a subject. When that subject is a pronoun, it must be in the objective case.

- They found *Leonard lying* on the floor.
- They found *him lying* on the floor.

Case of Gerund Modifiers   In formal writing, the possessive case is used for gerund modifiers.

- Sean did not mind *my going*.
- I did not object to *Henry's performing* so badly.

If the modifier is in the plural or has no possessive form, the possessive is not used.

- The teachers hoped that the parents assisting at the rehearsal would not interfere too much in the *students rehearsing*.
- Can you conceive of the *party deciding* to run a candidate under the circumstances?

GET

The past participle of *get* is *got*, but *gotten* is also used in the present and past perfect and in informal English.

- What have you *got* (*gotten*) by those methods?
- He had *got* (*gotten*) past his final examinations and was ready for graduation.

GOBBLEDYGOOK

Gobbledygook is a term that describes euphemistic writing that goes around and around indefinitely, relying on high-flown terminology to confuse rather then enlighten the reader. This word originally referred to bureaucratic jargon, but now it is in common use to cover all kinds of circumlocution

George Orwell, in his essay "Politics and the English Language," cites a fictitious English professor who wants to justify Soviet totalitarianism. A simple statement of his position would be: "I believe in killing off your opponents when you can get good results by doing so." Unwilling, or congenitally unable, to make this straightforward statement, he writes instead:

> While freely conceding that the Soviet regime exhibits certain features which the humanitarian may be inclined to deplore, we must, I think, agree that a certain curtailment of the right to political opposition is an unavoidable concomitant of transitional periods, and that the rigors which the Russian people have been called upon to undergo have been amply justified in the sphere of concrete achievement.

This type of expression is all too common. Read any official statement by any group, or profession of beliefs by any political candidate, and you will be rewarded with a fresh supply of gobbledygook. If you want to make up your own, use the following lists of words. For a ready-made phrase that will amuse and impress, select one word from each column:

Column A	*Column B*	*Column C*
validated	preternatural	ambiance
incremental	salutary	dichotomy
syncretistic	exophthalmic	megalomania
recondite	cooperative	expertise
homologous	simplistic	rationale
ambivalent	ontogenetic	*modus operandi*
charismatic	demagogic	covenant
de facto	epicene	atrophy
medieval	vertiginous	*Weltschmerz*
a priori	ephemeral	symmetry

In your own writing, develop an alarm system that will prevent you from resorting to gobbledygook. The simple statement is always the clearest.

H

HANG

The past participle of *hang*, in the sense of execute, is *hanged*. In all other senses, it is *hung*.

- The men were *hanged* in the public square.
- Most artists have *hung* their own paintings in our show.

HE, SHE

Speakers and writers of English wanting to refer to both sexes are faced with the problem of reference with the pronouns *he* and *she*. It is common to use *he* regardless of the fact that a female may be part of the antecedent. A convenient way out for the timid is to cast sentences requiring this kind of reference in the plural.

- He announced that each employee would have to make *his* report in person. (This form is used commonly despite the fact that some of the employees are women.)
- He announced that all employees would have to make *their* reports in person.

Above all, do not resort to the clumsy:

- He announced that each employee would have to make his or her report in person.

HOMONYM

Homonyms are words that sound alike: *fair* and *fare*, *bear* and *bare*, *him* and *hymn*, *male* and *mail*.

HOWEVER

However is used both as a conjunctive adverb and as a parenthetic word. As a conjunctive adverb, it is most appropriate in formal English; in general English, it is usually replaced by *but* or by a semicolon. As a parenthetic word, *however* is used to help make a pair of sentences more coherent.

- They were willing to accept all the honors that went with the appointment; *however*, they were not willing to do any of the work.
- Several of the sheep made straight for the far corner of the field. One, *however*, veered off and had to be turned by the collie.

The third use of *however* is as an adverb.

- *However* hard you try, you will not find the key.

More and more, *however* is being used to bridge two sentences, as in the first example above, but with *however* as the first word of the second sentence. This use is relatively new and is abhorrent to many teachers and editors.

HYPHEN

The hyphen is a mark that indicates the division of words at the end of a line of type or manuscript, splices words together to form compounds, and separates vowels when certain prefixes are added to words that begin with a vowel.

Word Division Most teachers and editors would rather read pages of manuscript that have jagged right-hand margins than wonder whether the writer intended to end a line neatly by dividing a word or whether he thought good spelling required a hyphen. When you must divide a word at the end of a line, the hyphen is required. Divide between double consonants. Divide between syllables as long as both parts of the words are pronounceable. Never divide when only one letter will be left on a line. Never divide a word of one syllable.

Compound Words Many English words have passed through three stages in their development: first as two or more separate words, then as hyphenated words, and finally as single words. For example, almost all ball games were separate words, such as foot ball, base ball, and basket ball, before they reached their modern spellings. Many words have retained their hyphens, stopping at the second stage of development—especially if the first part of the word is not a simple modifier of the other: Anglo-American, secretary-treasurer. The dictionary is the arbiter in matters of this kind.

A hyphen divides numerals from twenty-one to ninety-nine; compounds of self, as in self-oriented and self-centered; family relationships, as in mother-in-law, daughter-in-law, and sister-in-law; and two-word adjectives, particularly when one of the words is an adverb.

- third-class stateroom, easy-moving bearings

A hyphen is used with a numeral that is part of a modifier.

- 6-foot boards, 10-inch beams

A hyphen is used with a letter linked to a noun.

- X-ray, I-beam

A hyphen is used with many adverb-adjective modifiers when the adverb does not end in -ly.

- well-traveled, slow-growing, late-blooming

The hyphen is dropped when the modifier is in the predicate position.

- This lettuce is late blooming.
- Route 87 is well traveled.

When a group of words is conceived as a unit, hyphens are usually required.

- devil-may-care attitude, out-and-out bounder

But *nevertheless, heretofore,* and many others are single, unhyphenated words.

Prefixes To avoid ambiguities in pronunciation, as when two *e*'s or two *o*'s are brought together, a hyphen is often used:

- re-enter, re-examine, co-operate

This practice too is passing. With the virtual disappearance of the cooper's art, for example, there is little danger in spelling *co-operate* as *cooperate*. Notice that we once used the *dieresis* to differentiate short and long vowels that occur in sequence: reëxamine, coöperate. Unless you are blessed with a German typewriter, you will have trouble finding a key that can make a dieresis.

The hyphen is retained in words that would cause confusion if the hyphens were omitted: recreation and re-creation, recollect and re-collect. Such pairs have entirely distinct meanings, and the hyphens bear a large responsibility.

The hyphen is used with stressed prefixes, such as *ex* and *all*.

- ex-Governor, all-Conference

(Do not confuse the Latin *ex*, a preposition, with the English prefix *ex*. No hyphen is used in such Latin expressions as *ex officio* and *ex post facto*.)

The hyphen is the most provoking of all marks of punctuation, for its uses are so varied that few writers and editors can remember them all. If you use a dictionary as authority on questions of hyphenation, be sure to use only one dictionary. If you want to have the best authority on your side in a hyphen dispute, use the United States Government Printing Office Style Manual, which devotes over fifty pages to punctuation and is generally considered by American writers to be The Last Word.

IDIOM

An idiom is an expression whose meaning is different from the literal interpretation of the words within it.

- The orchestra played sluggishly until the final movement, when it caught fire and brought the house down. (Can you imagine the reaction of a foreign reader to this sentence?)

But all languages have their idioms. When the French want to say relatively simple things, they resort to expressions that drive young American students wild.

Idioms are important writing tools, but they tend to become overworked. At that stage they are *old hat* (a cliche) and *should be dropped* (slang), along with *caught fire* and *brought the house down*.

IF

If is a subordinating conjunction that introduces a condition.

- If he applies, he will get the job.
- If its food is good, a restaurant will prosper.
- All trees will thrive in this climate, if the garden catalogue is to be believed.
- If you can keep your head about you. . . .

Whether is used in place of *if* with expressions of doubt and with indirect questions, in combination with *or*. *If* is not used with *or* in formal English:

- He does not know whether he will go or stay.
- We cannot tell whether we are correct or not.
- We cannot tell whether we are correct.

IMAGERY

Imagery is a word or group of words that appeals to the senses. Most poetry, and a good deal of prose, uses imagery constantly to heighten meaning by appealing to the senses, supplementing the purely intellectual appeal of exposition. Yeats's "bee-loud glade" appeals to sound, sight, touch, smell, and—if we associate bees with honey—taste.

Writers should use imagery, but not if the images are trite. Poor writers will often attempt to decorate their prose by resorting to what are inevitably poor images, invented by others and long ago discarded. Your images should come from your own experience. In the passage below, from *Walden*, see how Thoreau uses images from common experience. There is nothing exotic that he could not have experienced himself (at least second-hand, in the case of Sparta).

> I wanted to live deep and suck out all the marrow of life, to live so sturdily and Spartan-like as to put to rout all that was not life, to cut a broad swath and shave close, to drive life into a corner, and reduce it to its lowest terms, and, if it proved to be mean, why then to get the whole and genuine meanness of it, and publish its meanness to the world....

IMPLY, INFER

The confusion between *imply* and *infer* has become a national joke as the airwaves and the printed page become more and more cluttered by the efforts of the quasi-literate. But this is not the only pair of words that has suffered so. *Uninterested* and *disinterested* have gone the same way. The ability to keep these two pairs separate is almost a mark of caste today.

The initiator *implies,* the receiver *infers*. Thus, the writer and the speaker will *imply,* the reader and listener *infer*. In the general language, as implied above, the distinction between these two words no longer exists. In all your formal writing, be sure to observe the difference in meaning.

INDICATIVE MOOD

The indicative mood is the usual form of English verbs in clauses and sentences. It makes an assertion or asks a question.

- The streets through which the procession *went were lined* with spectators who *watched* with delight.
- Why *have* you *found* it necessary to lie?
- Where *will* we *be* one hundred years from now?

Some grammarians mistakenly assert that the indicative mood is used to state facts. Many a lie has been told in the indicative mood.

INDIRECT DISCOURSE

In indirect discourse, we paraphrase or summarize in our own words the writing or speech of someone else. In report writing, indirect discourse saves space and time and usually represents an improvement in style compared with verbatim quotation.

Direct "The crowds that lined the streets were inclined to behave well. There was much noise from horns, cowbells, frying pans, firecrackers, etc., but no serious disorder."

Indirect Well-behaved crowds lined the streets, and although there was a good deal of noise, there were no incidents.

Whether you quote or paraphrase depends on the language of the original and on your purpose in introducing the material. If you can paraphrase in fewer words than the original and not lose its tone or intent, then paraphrase. If the original is written as well as possible, and if the full quotation is useful to your exposition, then quote. Of course, even though indirect discourse does not employ quotation marks, you must nevertheless cite the source.

INFINITIVE

The infinitive is the unbounded root form of the verb, the form found in the dictionary, usually preceded by *to*: to *sit*, to *walk*, to *run*. Infinitives can have active or passive voice and simple or progressive tense:

	Active		*Passive*
	Simple	*Progressive*	
Present	to walk	to be walking	to be walked
Perfect	to have walked	to have been walking	to have been walked

The present infinitive indicates time that is the same or future to the time of the main verb.

- It is pleasant *to walk* with you.
- The enemy is willing *to talk* with you.

The perfect infinitive indicates time that is previous to the time of the main verb.

- I was happy *to have walked* with you.

Infinitive Without To   *To* can be omitted after such verbs as *can, do, dare, go, try,* and *come.*

- He would rather *go*. He can *go* when he wants.
- Do you dare *come* without him? He does *try* from time to time.

Other verbs take the infinitive form with or without *to*.

- You really helped him *swim*. You really helped him *to swim*.

Infinitive of Linking Verb   Usage is divided over the case of the pronoun after the infinitive of a linking, or copulative, verb. In general English, the objective case is used; in formal English, the subjective case is used.

General   I supposed it to be *him*.

Formal   I supposed it to be *he*.

The infinitive can be used in absolute constructions.

- *To lead* the armed forces in the offensive, all units were put under unified command.

INFORMAL ENGLISH

Informal English—the language we use in narrative, in informal talks, and in discussion—is rarely appropriate in general or formal English. The use of informal English interspersed in general or formal discourse is conspicuous because it clashes with the main body of expression. Such lack of consistency is poor style. If you need to find a general or formal expression to replace an informal expression, use your dictionary or thesaurus.

IT

It is the neuter third person singular pronoun. When *it* functions as a pronoun with a clearly recognizable antecedent, the word presents no problem. *It* does present a stylistic problem in the common constructions *it is* and *it was*.

- *It was* there that he found peace.

In this sentence, emphasis is lost by having the logical subject *he* buried as the subject of the *that* clause. Unless the writer is striving for some rhythmic effect, the sentence should be:

- He found peace there.

Examine your writing for *it is, it was, there is, there are* constructions. How many of them can you justify?

ITS, IT'S

Its is the possessive pronoun. It does not have an apostrophe.

- Seven of *its* offspring went on to win major show awards.
- He wanted to be sure that the house retained *its* scrubbed appearance until a receptive buyer was found.

It's is the contraction for *it is* and *it has*.

- *It's* a long, long way to Tipperary.
- *It's* been a long time.

IT'S I, IT'S ME

The argument over *it's I, it's me* has its roots in the problem of the case of a pronoun following a linking verb. In formal English, the subjective case is used; in general English, usage is divided. In speech, almost all of us say *it's me*, and most grammarians accept this. Similarly, we say *it is him* rather than the formal *it is he*. Resolve your uncertainty by asking yourself whether general or formal language is appropriate to the situation.

[IT] 67

J

JARGON

Jargon is highly specialized language peculiar to a trade or profession, but avoided in writing and speech by careful practitioners of that profession. Jargon is misuse of language marked by substitution of abstract words for concrete, overuse of long and specialized words, and reliance on words that do not contribute to meaning.

K

KIND OF, SORT OF

Kind and *sort* agree in number with the noun that follows. The demonstrative adjective that precedes *kind* and *sort* must also agree in number.

- *This kind* of biscuit sells well throughout England.
- *These kinds* of biscuits sell well throughout England.
- *This sort* of foolishness must stop.
- *Those sorts* of fellows always make enemies wherever they go.

KIND OF A, SORT OF A

Avoid *kind of a* and *sort of a* in formal writing. Although these constructions are frequently heard, they are not acceptable in formal or informal writing.

We may say:

- He was that kind of a person.

But we write:

- He was that kind of person.

L

LAY, LIE

Lay is a transitive verb, which means that it can take an object. *Lie* is an intransitive verb, which means that no action is transmitted from the subject.

- If you are tired, why don't you *lay* down your load?
- If you are tired, why don't you *lie* down?

The principal parts of the two verbs are:

- lay, laid, lain
- lie, lay, lain

These verbs give us trouble because the past tense of *lie* has the same form as the present of *lay*. Distinguish carefully the different meanings of these two forms, and you will have no trouble.

LEARN, TEACH

In nonstandard English, *learn* is sometimes used in place of *teach*, but in general English these two verbs have quite different meanings, demonstrated by these examples:

- Jody *learned* more that afternoon than he had been able to learn in his life until then.
- His father *taught* him to harrow the land carefully before planting.

LESS, FEW

Less refers to things measured (amount), *few* to things counted.

- *Few* people are aware of all the preparations necessary before a Broadway performance.
- Many people have urged that the mass media put *less* emphasis on violence.

LEAVE, LET

Leave is sometimes used in nonstandard English in place of *let*, a substitution which is incorrect in standard English.

Incorrect *Leave* me go!
Correct *Let* me go!
Incorrect She told the bully to *leave* them alone.
Correct She told the bully to *let* them alone.

LEVEL

Level (of diction) is a term frequently used by teachers to indicate that a word or phrase so marked is inappropriate in the given context. It should be replaced with a more appropriate expression. When in doubt about the acceptability of a word in the general language, consult your dictionary.

LIGHTED, LIT

Both *lighted* and *lit* are used for the past tense and the past participle of *light*. *Lighted* is used more frequently as the adjective: the *lighted* causeway. *Lit* is used more frequently as the simple past: He *lit* the campfire.

LIKE, AS

Grammarians seem to be fighting a losing battle in their effort to keep distinct the functions of *like* and *as*. *Like* is a preposition, *as* a conjunction.

- The suit fits *like* a glove.
- He promised to stay *as* long *as* he could.

Like is being used increasingly as a conjunction—especially in place of *as if*—but such usage is confined to informal English.

- Samuel looked *like* he would never get up from the deck.

The beginning writer, who uses *like* as a subordinating conjunction through ignorance rather than preference, is best advised to treat *like* and *as* in the traditional manner. The advertising business and other linguistically influential groups can experiment all they want, but college teachers are not eager to give up the distinction between these two words.

LINKING VERB

A *linking*, or *copulative*, *verb* is one that makes a relationship between a subject and the adjective or noun that follows the verb. The most frequently used linking verb is *be*. Others are *feel, seem, prove, look, taste,* and *appear*.

- He *was* ill.
- She *seemed* well when we saw her last week.
- The captain *proved* a valuable friend in later years.
- Her desserts *taste* as desserts should.
- The audience *appeared* ready to fall asleep during the first act.

Many of these verbs can also take an object.

- He *felt* the wall behind him.
- Sally *proved* her solution by doing the problem another way.
- The butler *tasted* the wine before serving it.

LOAN, LEND

Loan is a noun, *lend* a verb. In general American speech, however, *loan* is regularly used as a verb.

General   The banker *loaned* me the money.
Formal   The banker *lent* me the money.

LOWER CASE

Teachers and editors use the abbreviation *l.c.* or draw a line through a capital letter to indicate that *lower case* (small letters) should be used in place of *upper case* (capital letters).

M

MIXED USAGE

Mixed usage is a term used to describe the common error of mixing different levels of usage: words or structures from informal writing used in formal writing, nonstandard words used in general writing. Once these errors are pointed out by a teacher or editor, the writer usually understands why the locution is inappropriate. Yet he may ask, "How am I to know something is inappropriate when I am writing it?" A question of this sort is difficult to answer, but some help is possible if the writer will read his work aloud slowly, listening to every word. If anything suspicious is heard, then the dictionary will establish the level of usage for a word. If the writer cannot find a substitute word in his own vocabulary, the thesaurus will help. Experience in writing and wide reading will gradually improve the diction of the writer and eliminate mixed usage.

MODAL AUXILIARIES

Modal auxiliaries are those words that "help" other verbs and they always occur with other verbs. They have no compound forms. The most common modal auxiliaries are *can, could; may, might; must, ought; shall, should; will, would*.

MODIFIERS

Modifiers are words or groups of words that limit, describe, or make more specific any of the main sentence elements. One of the main problems with modifiers is that writers fail to place them close enough to the words they modify. In the following examples, the modifiers are italicized:

> *Incorrect* The infield is designed *for a right-hand thrower, with the exception of first base.*

Correct   With the exception of first base, the infield is designed for a right-hand thrower.

Correct   The infield, *with the exception of first base*, is designed *for a right-hand thrower*.

Incorrect   Meeting the agent early, the dinner was over *in half an hour*.

Correct   Since we met the agent early, the dinner was over *in half an hour*.

In these sentences, as in most sentences, the article *the* is used freely. When you consider that an article is a modifier and that you would confuse your readers hopelessly by moving *the* freely within a sentence, you must see that all modifiers must be treated with the same respect.

MOOD

Mood refers to the changes in the form of a verb to denote the attitude of the writer toward the statement he is making. English employs the indicative, subjunctive, and imperative moods.

Indicative   He *remained* silent. (statement)

Indicative   Did he *remain* silent? (question)

Subjunctive   If he *were* here, I am sure he would not remain silent on this question. (condition contrary to fact)

Subjunctive   If only he *were* here, things would go better. (wish)

Subjunctive   The meeting will go more smoothly, provided he *pay* close attention to the business at hand. (supposition)

Subjunctive   Let peace *come* to all the world! (exhortation)

Imperative   *Leave* this room at once! (command)

Imperative   Please *stay* in your seats until the examination is over. (strong request)

MORPHEME

The smallest meaningful unit in the language is called a *morpheme*. It applies to words and to units that may combine with words: *-ing, -s, -ed, -ness, -ly, un-, im-*, etc.

MOST

Most is colloquial when used in the sense of *almost, nearly,* or *very.*

> *Correct*   He was *nearly* exhausted.
> *Correct*   He was *almost* exhausted.
> *Incorrect*   He was *most* exhausted.

Most has its proper usage as the superlative form of *more*. In the incorrect example above, there is no question of degrees of exhaustion. Exhaustion is one of those states like *dead*—one can be nearly dead, one can be almost dead, but one cannot be most dead! Once one reaches the point of exhaustion, one can go no further.

MS

The abbreviation for manuscript is MS; the abbreviation for manuscripts is MSS. Neither abbreviation carries a period.

MYSELF

Myself is one of a group of reflexive pronouns that intensify the pronoun or noun to which they refer.

- I *myself* will do all the work.
- I will do all the work *myself.*
- Joe is going to do the work *himself.*

N

NECESSARY

The word *necessary* is frequently misspelled. One *c* and two *s*'s.

NICE

In general and informal writing, the word *nice* has lost its meaning and should be avoided. Substitute more precise words.

> *Avoid* He is a *nice* fellow. (Just what do we mean here besides a general feeling that the fellow is not evil?)
>
> *Improved* He is a pleasant companion and generous to strangers.

NO-COMPOUNDS

Nobody, nowhere, nothing, none are written as one word. *Nobody, nothing,* and *none* are usually treated as singulars, but *none* is plural in all but educated speech and writing.

- Nobody knew *his* lesson.
- None *was* found.
- None *were* found.
- None of the witnesses *was* found.
- None of the witnesses *were* found.

NOHOW

When you say or write *nohow*, you are being jocular or are reporting speech by someone who would use such a nonstandard expression.

- "He couldn't do the problem nohow."

NONSTANDARD ENGLISH

Nonstandard English is language unacceptable in general and formal expression. In all cases, except quotation from nonstandard sources, use standard English.

NOUN

The noun is that part of speech that names a person, place, thing, or abstraction. It generally forms its plural in *-s* and the possessive with an apostrophe: *trees, Frank's wife.* Nouns function as subject, object, object of a preposition, appositive, subjective complement, modifier, indirect object, or possessive.

NOUN CLAUSE

A noun clause is a clause that functions as a noun. In many instances noun clauses are direct objects of such verbs as *believe, think, hope,* and *dream.* Other noun clauses function as subject or as object of a preposition. Most noun clauses are introduced by *that,* others by *who, whether,* and other conjunctions and pronouns.

- She hoped *that they would arrive on time.*
- *That Jose learned to swim in three weeks* pleased the coach.
- He was certain of *what he had heard.*

NOWHERE NEAR

The expression *nowhere near* is informal usage. In general and formal English, it is avoided.

Informal   We got *nowhere near* the top.
General   We did not get *near* the top.

NUMBER

Number is the grammatical concept of singular and plural for nouns, pronouns, and verbs. Number is an important consideration in reference and agreement.

- One of the boys who were approaching graduation has found trigonometry an insurmountable obstacle. (The verb *has found* agrees in number with *one*, its subject. The verb *were approaching* agrees in number with the pronoun *who*, its subject. We know that *who* is plural, because its antecedent is *boys*, a plural.)

Note that the word *number* is a collective noun, taken as a singular or as a plural according to the intention of the writer.

- A number of the playwrights *were denied* access to the library. (Here *number* is a synonym for a few.)
- The number of his accomplishments *is* rather impressive. (Here *number* is considered as a unit.)

O

OBJECT

Nouns and pronouns function as objects of verbs, prepositions, verbals, and certain adjectives.

Object of the Verb

He gave a *broom* to the society.

They found the *solution* difficult.

He wished *that they would leave* so he could get on with his work.

Object of Preposition

to the *movies,* on the *shelf,* from *what he could gather*

Object of Verbal

Corky loved to run the *mile.*

Jane liked swimming the *river* before breakfast.

Object of Adjective

The automobile was not worth the *price.*

ONE

One is a pronoun that can be used personally or impersonally. It can cause trouble in two ways: awkward repetition and faulty number of the verb.

- *One* can only ask for things *one* wants badly if *one* is to have any hope of getting what *one* wants.

This awkward example should not suggest that you may not use *one* at all. In fact, *one* is often used, but notice the way *one* is combined with other pronouns in the next two examples:

- *One* has to get *his* own way once in a while.

- *One* has to be true to *himself* if *he* is to look at *himself* in the mirror each morning.

One is often used with a plural in a modifying prepositional phrase, as in *one of those who*. The referent of *who* is plural in this construction, but modern writing tends to ignore this condition more and more. Whether the change in practice is due to sloppiness or to a deliberate effort is not known, but the *New York Times* and other publications of high standing appear to be ignoring the old requirements of agreement and reference.

Formal   Sherman was *one* of those *who* made clear *their stands* on the nomination.

General   Sherman was *one* of those *who* made clear his stand on the nomination.

You can be certain that your teachers will prefer the formal practice in regard to *one of those who*.

ONLY

In formal English, *only* is placed directly next to the construction modified.

- He has *only* three weeks left before he reports for induction. (To say *he only has* would imply that he has nothing else.)
- *Only* one electric light bulb was left intact after the vandals finished their work. (Just think of the change in meaning if the sentence read: One electric light bulb was left intact only after the vandals finished their work; *or,* One electric light bulb was left intact after the vandals finished their only work.)

In some cases, of course, the position of the word *only* can change in a limited way.

- Such words are used *only* in formal English.
- Such words are *only* used in formal English.
- Such words are used in formal English *only*.

While English generally is a demanding language, we are not bound completely. The important question to answer in regard to style is:

Where must I put modifiers to achieve precisely the effect I want to achieve?

OR

Or is a coordinating conjunction used to join two independent clauses or connect two grammatically similar elements.

Conjunction

We can all go in one car, *or* you can take your car and I will take mine.

Connective

Either Jonathan *or* Daniel will call for you.

We can take the luggage with us *or* send it on ahead.

They decided to give either their money *or* their paintings to the charity.

When *or* connects two elements used together as subject, the verb agrees with the number of the unit closer to it.

- Two short novels or one long one *is* required.
- One long novel or two short ones *are* required.

Or frequently combines with the words *either* and *and*.

- *Either* you stay *or* I will.
- *Either* both cars are repaired *or* none is.

Or is so frequently combined with *and* in business and technical writing that some have proposed the new word *andor* to replace the stopgap *and/or* that appears so often that dictionaries are beginning to list it without disapproval.

- Failure of the odometer *and/or* the speedometer will not help the driver.
- Failure of the odometer *andor* the speedometer will not help the driver.

In this case, as in almost all other cases of this type, the writer could have made his point well enough by using *or* alone. In formal English, a writer would have been able to express himself without either of the new locutions.

- Failure of the speedometer or the odometer or both will not help the driver.

ORGANIZATION

After *clarity*, the mark *organization* is the English teacher's most damning label. This criticism usually appears because the writer has not taken the time to outline his paper before beginning to write or, if he is not given to outlining, has not bothered to read his paper in rough draft to see whether it makes a tight, coherent statement.

OUT-OF CONSTRUCTIONS

Structures containing *out of* are hyphenated only when they are used as modifiers.

- That book is out of date. (The *out of* construction is a predicate adjective, not a modifier.)
- Some people thought that the Lawrenceville stories were out-of-date accounts of a dead age. (*Out-of-date* modifies accounts.)

Remember that *out-of* constructions are hyphenated when they precede the element modified, are not hyphenated when they follow it.

P

PARAGRAPH

Teachers use the word *paragraph*, the abbreviation *par.*, or the symbol ¶ when they want to indicate a mistake in paragraphing.

A paragraph represents the adequate development of an idea worthy of segregation in a stylistic unit of several sentences. The length of a paragraph cannot be stated precisely. Ideas are of different importance, and the length of a paragraph will be proportional to the simplicity or complexity of the idea expressed. If the idea is complex, most modern writers avoid the interminable paragraphs that were fashionable seventy-five years ago. They recognize that the attention span of the reader has its own limitations, so they break their development of an idea into digestible segments of several paragraphs coherently linked.

There is increasingly a tendency to make paragraphs extremely short—a pair of sentences or even one sentence alone. This practice may be all right for readers of tabloid newspapers, but it is difficult to believe that anything can be accomplished toward improving the style of formal papers by so limiting paragraphs. In fact, the reader of such short paragraphs must feel like the referee in a tennis match rather than an interested audience in search of mature ideas.

PARALLEL CONSTRUCTION

Elements performing similar grammatical functions should have similar grammatical forms.

Faulty Parallelism The educational system often overtaxes such teachers with large classes, outdated textbooks, and with doing excessive clerical work.

Correct Parallelism The educational system often overtaxes such teachers with large classes, outdated textbooks, and excessive clerical work.

Faulty Parallelism   The architect proposed a school far superior in design, more elaborately equipped, and that was better in regard to location than any other school in the district.

Correct Parallelism   The architect proposed a school far superior in design, equipment, and location than any other school in the district.

Faulty Parallelism   Most of the students and the girls in the school were enthusiastic about the project.

Correct Parallelism   Most of the male and female students were enthusiastic about the project.

PARAPHRASE

A paraphrase is a restatement in one's own words of the expression of another writer. Paraphrase differs from direct quotation in two ways: the words must be your own, and the paraphrase should be shorter than the original. Of course, it must be faithful to the meaning of the original. If a paraphrase is used for a class paper or for publication, the source of the original should be cited in a footnote.

PARENTHESES

Parentheses are used to separate material from a sentence when the material is too far removed from the general subject under discussion to be enclosed in commas or dashes. Additions, parenthetic expressions, and informative asides are punctuated by parentheses.

> Or what is there apart from the traditions of dungeoned warriors and kings (which will not wholly account for it) that makes the White Tower of London tell so much more strongly on the imagination of a traveled American. . . .
>
> —Melville, *Moby Dick*

> The young soldier returned to Rivière du Loup (Wolf River), where he had a small homestead.

> Insofar as Kipling grasps this, he simply sets it down to "the intense selfishness of the lower classes" (his own phrase).
>
> —Orwell, "Rudyard Kipling"

Parentheses are used to enclose references included in the text of a research paper.

> Lady Gregory said that if the reception of the play improved, it would come off on Saturday, but if it did not, it would be played until it received a fair hearing (*Irish Independent,* Feb. 1, 1907).

Parentheses enclose the place and date of publication in a footnote.

> Jack Kerouac, *Doctor Sax* (New York, 1959), p. 54.

Parentheses are sometimes used to enclose numbers or letters in an enumeration within a text: (1), (2); (a), (b).

PARTICIPLES

A participle is a verbal adjective having both past and present forms and active and passive voice.

	Active	*Passive*
Present	cleaning	being cleaned
Past	cleaned	having been cleaned

The forms and voices of the participle either can be used as modifiers or can combine with verbs.

Modifier The forms and voices of the participle are used as modifiers in a variety of constructions.

- *Encouraged* by their initial success, the authors started another book.
- The *smiling* candidate answered the loaded question, unaware that he was about to doom his candidacy.

Introductory participles refer to the subject of the sentence.

Incorrect *Closing* the paragraph, the force of lightning is compared with the force of water.

Correct *Closing* the paragraph, the author compared the force of lightning with the force of water.

Incorrect   Looking at the sun through the window of a heated room, it may seem warm outside when it is not.

Correct   Looking at the sun through the window of a heated room, you may think it is warm outside when it is not.

Absolute Construction   Absolute constructions—usually a noun modified by a participle—have only a general relationship to the rest of the sentence.

- *The principal checkpoints having been passed*, the group dispersed without further interference.

This type of construction is practically a direct translation from the Latin ablative absolute, beloved by Caesar, and so tends to be excessively formal or literary. Most often we change a construction such as the one above and place the absolute in a subordinate clause:

- *When the principal checkpoints had been passed*, the group dispersed without further interference.

Loosely related introductory participial phrases are also classified as absolutes.

- *Judging by his face*, he must be very young.
- *Taking all the circumstances into account*, the action was just.

Element of Verb Form   The present participle is used with the verb *be* to form progressive tenses.

- He *is beckoning* to you from across the street.
- She *was racing* to the finish line when a gust of wind turned her abeam.

The past participle is used with the verb *be* to form the passive voice.

- The incumbent *is favored* to win by a wide margin
- The guest speaker *was delayed* at the airport.

PASSIVE VERBS

Passive verbs are formed by the past participle and the appropriate form of the verb *be*. Passive verbs do not transfer action from the subject to

[PA]   87

some other sentence element, but indicate the manner in which the subject is itself acted upon.

In grammatical terms, if we think of the element receiving the action of a verb as the *logical object,* then the subject of a passive verb is a *logical object* occupying the *grammatical subject* position. In turn, the *logical subject* occupies a position as object of a preposition following the verb, or it does not appear at all. Examine the following sentence:

- The ball was hit by the man.

Who is performing the action? The *man*. What about the *ball*? The *ball* is being hit. So the *ball*, the logical object, is in the subject position, and the verb is therefore passive. In the active voice, the sentence would read:

- The man hit the ball.

The passive voice, then, shifts the emphasis from the logical subject to the logical object. This shift of emphasis is sometimes of great use in writing—particularly when we are writing of things that are happening *to* someone or something, rather than writing about *who is doing something to someone*. Much of the writing in science logically falls into this category.

On the other hand, thoughtless use of the passive often results in awkward, unemphatic sentences. In the following example, the passive voice is used in the first sentence to emphasize the focus of the writer's attention, the eminent sociologist Durkheim. In the second sentence, the emphasis shifts from the logical subject, *Durkheim*, in a manner that makes the reader wonder why we are no longer interested primarily in Durkheim:

> By 1887 Durkheim *was recognized* in the field as an outstanding sociologist, and he began his thirty-year university career. At the University of Bordeaux, a course in the social sciences *was created* for him.
>
> Adapted from Kardiner & Preble,
They Studied Man (New York, 1951),
p. 110.

Would we not have benefited from recasting the second sentence in the active voice so that our attention would still be directed at *Durkheim*, the logical subject? Now the pair of sentences would read:

By 1887 Durkheim *was recognized* in the field as an outstanding sociologist, and he began his thirty-year university career. At the University of Bordeaux, he *initiated* a course in the social sciences that *had been created* especially for him.

Notice that there is no stylistic rule against mixing active and passive verbs. The original selection already had the active verb *began* in the second independent clause of the first sentence. In the rewritten sentences, this active verb is retained, the independent clause of the second sentence is given an active verb, and the new subordinate clause is given the passive verb *had been created*. Through these changes we have achieved our stylistic purpose: to concentrate on the logical subject *Durkheim* throughout. We should use the passive *only* when we wish to emphasize the thing affected. Consider in this sentence:

- Three hundred civilians were killed.

It is the fate of the civilians we are interested in, not the means by which they were killed or what caused their deaths. The choice between active and passive is determined by the element in the sentence we wish to emphasize.

PERSON

Pronouns are classified by *person* and *number*. *Person* identifies who is indicated by the pronoun, *number* whether the pronoun is singular or plural. Personal pronouns are the only ones that have elaborate inflectional systems; other pronouns change forms only for the objective and possessive cases.

First Person

Case	*Singular*	*Plural*
Subjective	I	we
Possessive	my, mine	our, ours
Objective	me	us

Second Person

Case	*Singular*	*Plural*
Subjective	you	you
Possessive	your, yours	your, yours
Objective	you	you

	Third Person			
	Singular			
Case	Masculine	Feminine	Neuter	Plural
Subjective	he	she	it	they
Possessive	his	her, hers	its	their, theirs
Objective	him	her	it	them

Verbs indicate person and number only for the third person singular of the present tense: *I wash; you wash; he, she,* or *it washes.* Nouns are third person and regularly inflect to indicate singular or plural.

PERSONIFICATION

Personification is the stylistic device of attributing human characteristics to abstract ideas, objects, or animals. Used more in poetry than in prose writing, personification is a worthwhile technique in the hands of a professional, but it is often awkward when undertaken by a beginning writer, who often resorts to cliches in his attempts to use personification. Thus, for him, *time is* always *flying, tyranny is crying out for vengeance,* and *the oppressed land is bleeding.*

Notice what a poet does with personification:

> When Time began to rant and rage,
> The measure of her flying feet
> Made Ireland's heart begin to beat;
> And Time bade all his candles flare
> To light a measure here and there;
>
> —Yeats, "To Ireland in the Coming Times"

Naturally, the prose writer rarely sustains personification to this extent. Here is a portion of a speech by Mark Twain dealing with New England weather:

> There is a sumptuous variety about the New England weather that compels the stranger's admiration—and regret. The weather is always doing something there; always attending strictly to business; always getting up new designs and trying them on people to see how they will go. But it gets through more business in spring than in any other season. In the spring I have counted

one hundred and thirty-six different kinds of weather inside of twenty-four hours.

PHENOMENON, PHENOMENA

Phenomenon is singular, *phenomena* plural. Phenomenon originally meant *any object directly discernible through sight, smell, taste, etc.,* but the meaning has been extended to include *an uncommon or abnormal person, thing, or occurrence*—an inexplicable fact. The adjective *phenomenal* is usually intended in this sense.

PHRASAL VERB

A phrasal verb is any verb formed by an auxiliary and an infinitive or past participle: *shall run, is pleased, has been searched*. Phrasal verbs are also called periphrastic verbs.

PHRASE

A phrase is a group of words that functions as subject or object in a sentence or as modifier of another sentence element and that does not contain a subject or predicate. There are four types of phrases, their names being taken from the types of words of which they are composed: prepositional, participial, infinitive, and gerund.

Prepositional and participial phrases always function as modifiers. Infinitive phrases can function as modifiers or as subjects or objects. Gerund phrases always function as subjects or objects.

Prepositional Phrase   A prepositional phrase is composed of a preposition and its object.

- He came *out of his house*, went *to the store*, and bought a box *of cookies*.

The first two prepositional phrases function as adverbs (modifying *came* and *went*), and the third functions as an adjective (modifying *box*).

Participial Phrase   A participial phrase is composed of either the present or past participle, its object (if there is one), and any modifiers belonging to the unit.

- *Running to the window,* he saw the car leave the road and jump the curb.
- *Defeated in its third consecutive election,* the party decided to disband.

This type of phrase can easily become a dangling modifier, or dangling participle, if the writer does not take care to attach the phrase to a recognizable sentence element. In the first example, *he* is *running to the window.* In the second, the *party* has been *defeated in its third consecutive election.*

Infinitive Phrase   An infinitive phrase is composed of an infinitive, its object (if there is one), and modifiers.

- *To return to his own room* seemed the only way for the freshman to please the Dean of Residence Halls.
- He decided *to order the shirt* and *forget the cost.*

In the first sentence, the infinitive phrase has a prepositional phrase as its modifier. The entire phrase *to return to his own room* functions as the subject of the sentence. In the second sentence, the two infinitive phrases act together as a compound object. Notice that *to* has been omitted from the second infinitive phrase, *forget the cost.*

Gerund Phrase   A gerund phrase is composed of a gerund, its object (if there is one), and any modifiers.

- *His winning the game* caused joy in Mudville.

This gerund phrase functions as subject of *caused.* Notice that the pronoun before the gerund is in the possessive case. We often see the pronoun in the objective case in nonstandard English: *Him winning the game caused joy in Mudville.* Such a construction cannot be used in a college paper unless it is part of a quotation.

PLAGIARISM

Plagiarism is taking the words or ideas of another and representing them as your own. Avoid any suggestion of plagiarism by citing sources for the concepts you present, if they are not completely your own.

PLENTY

Plenty still survives in general and formal English as a noun, but as a modifier it is colloquial and should be avoided. Such sentences as *This is plenty good enough* and are not permissible in college themes.

PLURAL FORMS OF NOUNS

Nouns in English—with certain exceptions—form their plurals by adding *s* to the singular: *car, cars; horse, horses; alley, alleys.*

Exceptions and Problems

1. Nouns that end in a sounded *s* or in a sound close to *s* form their plurals by adding an extra syllable pronounced *es* so that the original ending can be heard. This includes nouns ending in *ch, dge, sh, ss,* and *z* sounds.

- church, churches; torch, torches; porch, porches
- hedge, hedges; sludge, sludges
- lash, lashes; sash, sashes
- mass, masses; cutlass, cutlasses
- adze, adzes; fuzz, fuzzes

2. For nouns ending in *y* preceded by a consonant, change the *y* to *i* and add *es*.

- sky, skies; fry, fries; body, bodies; belfry, belfries

Note that nouns ending in *y* preceded by a vowel form their plurals in the conventional way: bay, bays; alloy, alloys.

3. Certain nouns ending in *o* preceded by a consonant form the plural by adding *es*.

- tomato, tomatoes; echo, echoes; mosquito, mosquitoes

Other nouns ending in *o* preceded by a consonant form the plural by adding *s*.

- canto, cantos; solo, solos; tremolo, tremolos

Certain nouns ending in *o* preceded by a consonant have both plural forms.

- zero, zeroes, zeros; cargo, cargoes, cargos; hobo, hoboes, hobos

Since nouns ending in *o* preceded by a consonant vary in forming plurals, look up all doubtful words in a dictionary.

4. Some nouns ending in *f* or *fe* change the *f* to *v* and add *s* or *es*.

- calf, calves; elf, elves; half, halves; knife, knives

Other nouns ending in *f* have regular plurals.

- belief, beliefs; chief, chiefs; puff, puffs; roof, roofs

Note that *knife* as a noun is *knives* in the plural; the verb *knife* is *knifes* in the third person singular present, *knifing* in the present participle, and *knifed* in the past.

5. Certain nouns—primarily survivors from Anglo-Saxon, which was more fully inflected than English—form the plural by adding an *n* sound, or by changing a vowel, or by changing a vowel and the final consonant.

- child, children; ox, oxen
- man, men; woman, women; foot, feet
- louse, lice; mouse, mice

6. Some nouns have the same form in the singular and plural, and others have plural forms only and are construed as singular.

- deer, fish (sometimes fishes), moose, quail, sheep, vermin
- series, species, trousers, scissors, news

7. Many words of foreign origin retain the plural form of the language from which they were borrowed. As time goes by, some of these words are beginning to accept English endings. A few examples of common words with foreign plural endings are:

addendum, addenda
antithesis, antitheses
automaton, automata
axis, axes
basis, bases
crisis, crises
criterion, criteria
datum, data
ellipsis, ellipses
erratum, errata
genus, genera
graffito, graffiti
hypothesis, hypotheses
medium, media
metamorphosis, metamorphoses
minutia, minutiae
phenomenon, phenomena
radius, radii

This list would not be complete if it did not include:

- alumnus (male), alumna (female)
- alumni (male plural), alumnae (female plural)

PREDICATE

The predicate of a sentence or clause is the verb with its modifiers and direct and indirect object, or its complement. Together these elements make a statement with respect to the subject.

PREDICATE ADJECTIVE, PREDICATE NOMINATIVE

An adjective following a linking verb is called a predicate adjective; a noun following a linking verb is called a predicate nominative.

PREFIX

A prefix is a unit of one or more letters or syllables added to the beginning of a stem or word to form a new word. There are several dozen prefixes in active use in the English language: *a* as in amoral; *sub*, as in substandard; *pan*, as in pantheism; *poly*, as in polytheism; and *in*, as in inborn are some of these.

Suffixes are syllables added to the ends of words. Together, prefixes and suffixes are called *affixes*.

PREPOSITIONS AND PREPOSITIONAL PHRASES

A preposition shows the relationship of a noun or pronoun to another word in a sentence. A prepositional phrase is any group of words composed of a preposition, the object of the preposition, and the modifiers of that object.

- *to* the *movie*
- *on* the farthest *limb*
- *with* the utmost *ease*
- *across* the wide *part of* the *river*

Prepositional phrases are among the most widely used modifying structures in the language. Writers do not have trouble using prepositional phrases unless (1) they are confused about usage (different *from* or different *than*?) or (2) they use too many bulky prepositions (*in regard to, in case of*). General and formal usage prefer *different from;* and a good example of bulky prepositions marring a sentence is seen in this example:

- *For* what reason did you ask her to let you read *to* her *out of* the book?

Prepositions at the ends of sentences are a matter of concern to many teachers of English—generally teachers who have not kept their stylistic eyes open through the years. While we have all heard "we should not end a sentence with a preposition," English idiom and rhythm frequently demand that we do just that.

- In her extreme distress, she had no one to turn to. (Formal style might call for . . . *to whom to turn.*)
- He had no one to play with. (Formal style might call for . . .*with whom to play.* Of course, it is difficult to imagine a formal setting for a sentence with this meaning. Above all, however, we must not fall prey to such barbarisms as: *He had no one with whom to play with.*)

A clever way to dispose of the controversy over whether to end a sentence with a preposition is to quote Bertram Braley:

The grammar has a rule absurd
Which I would call an outworn myth:

96 [PR]

"A preposition is a word
You mustn't end a sentence with!"

PRINCIPAL, PRINCIPLE

If you cannot remember the spelling of these two words, you are not alone: confusion of *principal* and *principle* has reached epidemic proportions. To begin with the exceptions: *Principal* is the head of a school (probably because he once was the *principal teacher*), and *principals* own most of the stock in a company (probably because they once were *principal participants*). Remember *a* for adjective. *Principal* is an adjective, and *principle* is a noun.

- Our *principal* complaint is that the group seemed to have no *principles*.
- The *principal* witness in the case said that he was not concerned with the interest, but cared only about the *principal*.

PRINCIPAL PARTS OF VERB

The principal parts of a verb are the roots from which all other forms derive: infinitive, past, and past participle. Regular, or weak, verbs form the past and past participle by adding *ed* to the infinitive: *walk, walked, walked; love, loved, loved.* By adding auxiliary verbs, we can form all the tenses from these: *will walk, have walked, will have walked,* etc.

Irregular, or strong, verbs form the past and past participle by a vowel change, or by no change at all in at least one case: *bid, bid, bid* (in the sense of *offer*).

Here are some of the most common strong verbs:

begin	began	begun
blow	blew	blown
bring	brought	brought
choose	chose	chosen
come	came	come
dive	dived (dove)	dived
do	did	done
draw	drew	drawn
drink	drank	drunk

fly	flew	flown
forget	forgot	forgotten (forgot)
freeze	froze	frozen
get	got	got (gotten)
go	went	gone
know	knew	known
lie	lay	lain
ride	rode	ridden
ring	rang (rung)	rung
rise	rose	risen
run	ran	run
see	saw	seen
shrink	shrank (shrunk)	shrunk
sing	sang (sung)	sung
spring	sprang (sprung)	sprung
swim	swam	swum
swing	swung	swung
take	took	taken
throw	threw	thrown
write	wrote	written

If you are unsure of the principal parts of any verb, use your dictionary.

PROFESSOR

A person with the academic rank of assistant professor or above should be addressed as "Professor" in an academic setting. This includes letters other than personal ones. Use the abbreviation *Prof.* when writing out the full name; spell it out when using the last name alone.

- Prof. Andrew L. Eastwood; Professor Eastwood

If you give the full title of the professor, specify his professorial rank.

- Andrew L. Eastwood, Associate Professor of Oriental Literature

Since *professor* is an indication of rank, the term should not be applied to faculty members who are not professors. Before the name of an instructor, use *Mr., Mrs., Miss,* or *Ms.,* or *Dr.* if the instructor has a doctor's degree.

PROGRESSIVE VERBS

Progressive verbs are formed by the present participle and the appropriate form of the verb *be*. A progressive verb indicates that the action described is in progress at the time specified.

- He *is walking* the dog now.
- He *was walking* the dog when you called.
- He *had been walking* the dog for over an hour when the car appeared.
- He *will have been walking* the dog for over an hour and will be too tired to stop for a chat.

PRONOUN

Pronouns are words that take the place of nouns and perform all noun functions. They create difficulty because many of them have different forms in the subjective, objective, and possessive cases, and strong conventions exist for the use of these cases in certain constructions.

Personal Pronouns   Personal pronouns have different forms for the subjective, possessive, and objective cases.

		Subjective	*Possessive*	*Objective*
First Person	Singular	I	my, mine	me
	Plural	we	our, ours	us
Second Person	Singular	you	your, yours	you
	Plural	you	your, yours	you
Third Person	Singular	he, she, it	his, her, hers, its	him, her, it
	Plural	they	their, theirs	them

Relative Pronouns   The nominative and objective forms of relative pronouns cause writers the most trouble, often because the preposition and the relative pronoun used as object are widely separated: The boy *whom* you gave the bicycle *to* does not want it. Nobody would ever say *to whom you gave the bicycle,* but a careless speaker or writer might fall into: The boy *who* you gave the bicycle *to* does not want it.

Subjective	*Possessive*	*Objective*
who	whose	whom
that		that
which	whose	which

The relative pronouns are frequently combined with *ever:*

    whoever   whomever

Reflexive Pronouns Pronouns combined with *self* are reflexive—they refer to the subject and give it emphasis.

- I will do it *myself.* We do things *ourselves.*
- You *yourself* will have to do this. You do things *yourselves.*
- She does things *herself.* They *themselves* do not know.

Demonstrative Pronouns Demonstrative pronouns point out the person or thing referred to.

- *This* is no longer interesting. *That* will satisfy him.

In addition to the four main types of pronouns, there are interrogative pronouns—*who, which, what;* indefinite pronouns—*any, anyone, some, someone,* etc.; and reciprocal pronouns—*each other, one another.*

PROOFREADING

Proofreading is the last necessary step in the preparation of a manuscript. Before submitting a paper to an instructor or an editor, be sure to read slowly through the complete manuscript, checking for spelling, typing, pagination, and the like. Since every page is important, be sure to read the entire manuscript. For example, many errors of inconsistency are commonly found in bibliographies. When you consider how much time goes into writing and researching term papers and reports, surely the extra time needed for proofreading is a small expenditure.

PUBLIC

Public is a collective noun that takes either a singular or plural verb, depending on whether the word is intended as a single unit or as a collection of people.

- The public *is* often impatient for change.
- The public *are* often thought of as composed of different power groups.

This same reasoning holds true in determining the number of all collective nouns.

PUNCTUATION

A common misconception of beginning writers is that punctuation is determined merely by taste or by breath control. As a matter of fact, while there is some room for art in punctuating, specific rules govern most uses of the marks of punctuation. To make certain that your writing conforms to existing rules, check the entries under each of the marks and try to learn the rules as you read so that you will not have to check again and again.

Q

QUESTION MARK

A question mark is used at the end of a sentence that asks a question.

- Will you go home for the holidays?
- Are there any games left in the schedule?

If a sentence asking a question contains a quotation, the question mark is outside the quotation mark; if the quotation is itself a question, the question mark falls inside the quotation mark.

- Can you be certain under these circumstances that you did not say, "Other students demonstrated just for kicks"?
- He said, "Is there any doubt that the entire group was at fault?"

A question mark is also used to indicate that a date is uncertain.

- Julian of Norwich, born 1342(?), was a recluse in a cell attached to the Church of St. Julian at Norwich.
- Archimedes (287?-212 B.C.)

QUESTIONS

We normally use inverted word order in a sentence that asks a question: *Were you* late yesterday? (Subject follows verb.) This inverted order is also used with auxiliary verbs.

- *Can you meet* the class tomorrow?
- *Will you wait* for me?

Note that certain questions can also be expressed in normal word order:

- You do take wine after dinner?
- He really said that he was unable to attend?

This word order is more appropriate to speech than to writing, but it can appear in writing when questions are being quoted verbatim.

QUOTATION MARKS

Quotation marks are used to indicate that the material within them is quoted directly from another source. When there is a quotation within a quotation, single quotation marks are used for the internal quotation. Normally, both the single and double quotation marks come outside the final punctuation if both end there.

> "Writing to his friend William Erskine in 1796, Sir Walter Scott noted that many apologies for publication 'are in fact no apologies at all. Either the things are worth the attention of the public or they are not.'"
>
> <div style="text-align:right">Sir Walter Scott, <i>Life of John Dryden</i>,
Ed. Bernard Kreissman (University of
Nebraska Press, 1963), p. vii.</div>

Extensive Quotation When the quoted material is extensive—one rule of thumb is five typewritten lines or more—it is set off from the rest of the paper. The material is single spaced, indented, and not enclosed in quotation marks.

> Now, for the first time since the end of World War II, we may be approaching a point from which it will be possible to see the shape of a new European order to replace the system that was destroyed so blindly fifty years ago; it is perhaps not too much to say that the lights which went out for Sir Edward Grey in 1914 are flickering on again. At present the process of reconciliation between the two Europes is proceeding without effective American participation because of America's preoccupation with the Vietnamese war; the result of course is that the United States is being left behind and Western Europe's developing friendliness with Eastern Europe is beginning to separate Europe from America.
>
> <div style="text-align:right">J. William Fulbright, <i>The Arrogance of Power</i>
(New York, 1966), p. 216.</div>

Dialogue   Dialogue is set off in quotation marks. Every time the speaker changes, a new paragraph is required.

"Who is it, Jessie?"
"No one you know, Mom."

When the speaker is indicated, a comma is used in addition to the quotation marks.

- Maria said, "Half the trouble could have been averted if the authorities had arrived promptly."
- "Half the trouble could have been averted," Maria said, "if the authorities had arrived promptly."
- "Half the trouble could have been averted if the authorities had arrived promptly," Maria said.

Notice that *if* is not capitalized in the second example, since it is part of the sentence being quoted.

Titles   Quotation marks are used for the titles of works contained within other works—individual stories in a collection of short stories, magazine articles, chapters of a book, titles of poems in a collection of poetry—and for song titles.

- "The Gambler, the Nun, and the Radio" from *The Fifth Column and the First Forty-Nine Stories*
- "Yes and No" from *Selected Poems and Parodies*
- "John Henry" from *American Ballads and Folk Songs*

Note that the title of the larger work, from which the shorter work is cited, is printed in italics. Underscore such words in typewritten or handwritten papers to indicate that italics would be used in print.

Apologetic Quotes   Many writers follow the practice of enclosing an inappropriate word in quotation marks, thinking that this practice will make the word appropriate. It is far better to find the word that expresses the writer's intentions precisely. The mystique of quotation marks around a word does not always make clear to the reader just what is intended by the author.

R

REAL, REALLY

Real is an adjective, *really* an adverb. In informal English, real is often used as an adverb: You look *real* well. He is a *real* good guy. Such usage is not acceptable in papers written in general or formal English except when the word is part of material being quoted from the speech of someone who uses informal English.

REASON IS BECAUSE

After the construction *the reason is,* general and formal English require either a noun clause introduced by *that* or a noun. *The reason is because* is common in colloquial speech, but unacceptable in writing.

- The reason is that his mother will not let him apply.
- The reason is the indignant response of most voters.

REFERENCE OF PRONOUNS

Faulty reference of pronouns is one of the most common grammatical errors. The problem takes two forms—either a pronoun does not agree in number with its antecedent or there is no clearly visible antecedent for a pronoun.

- White America, during *its* westward expansion, basing *their* actions on furthering civilization, denied the Indian the freedom to roam his land. (The writer of this sentence could not make up his mind concerning the number of the phrase *White America.* He therefore elected to treat it first as a singular, then as a plural. The second pronoun should have been *its.*)
- Unless White America accepts Black equality and does not restrain *their* freedom, we shall not see peace in this generation. (What is the antecedent of *their*? One would suppose the writer

meant *Blacks,* but that word does not appear in the sentence. The sentence should be recast: Unless White America accepts the equality of Blacks and does not restrain *their* freedom, we shall not see peace in this generation.)

- The technique is called extended imagery, because it uses words that are carried from one sentence to another. (The pronoun *it* appears to have *technique* as its antecedent, but a technique cannot *use words*. The sentence can be rewritten in two ways: The technique is called extended imagery, because the writer uses words that are carried from one sentence to another. The technique is called extended imagery, because it is characterized by the use of words carried from one sentence to another.)

The best way to avoid the problem of faulty pronoun reference is to make certain that the pronoun is close to the word on which it depends. As you edit your own work, you will be able to determine whether a pronoun has the correct antecedent and whether the pronoun and antecedent agree in number.

RELATIVE CLAUSE

A relative clause is introduced by a relative pronoun or a relative adjective. The pronoun can often be omitted from a relative clause.

- The man *who talked to the Lions Club* is a friend of mine.
- He believed *that he would be home on time.*
- He believed *he would be home on time.*
- The ball *that we are now using* is cheaper than the old ball.
- The ball *we are now using* is cheaper than the old ball.

RELATIVE PRONOUN

A relative pronoun is used to refer to persons (*who, whom, whose, that*) or things (*which, that*).

- the girl *whom* I marry, the girl *that* I marry
- this sword, *which* is sharper than any other

REPETITION

Every teacher of writing has tried to make clear to perplexed students that repetition is not always bad style, that fastening on the proper word or expression and then using it as often as necessary is good style. Some grade school and high school teachers mistakenly encourage the use of the thesaurus for finding what turn out to be inappropriate synonyms.

Awkward Repetition   Repetition is awkward when it is unnecessary or when it does not add to meaning.

- It is through imagery that most poets convey meaning. And it is through this imagery that the student of poetry must find meaning.

The repetition of *it is through* is both awkward and unnecessary. The repetition of *meaning* is not necessary, nor is the repetition of *imagery*. The sentence should have been stated more succinctly:

- Poets convey meaning through imagery, and students must find it there.

Examine this excerpt from a student paper on Tolstoi's *The Death of Ivan Ilych*. Notice the awkward repetition of *phony*, which is a poor word in any case in a student paper:

Ivan's awareness is, in essence, his dissatisfaction with his past life. The first sign of this awareness, that man is a phony, occurs when Ivan consults his physician about his illness.... Ivan also recognized his wife and daughter as phonies when they discussed his health. This is in contrast with the pure Gerasim, who was not a phony but a real person.

The main problem with this kind of writing is that the reader is attracted to the awkward repetition of *phony* rather than to what the writer is saying; it becomes difficult to focus on the thought because of the manner in which it is expressed.

By way of contrast, examine these examples of repetition that increase understanding and heighten stylistic effectiveness:

- Victory at all costs, victory in spite of all terror, victory however long and hard the road may be; for without victory there is no survival.

- We shall fight on the beaches, we shall fight on the landing grounds, we shall fight in the fields and in the streets, we shall fight in the hills; we shall never surrender.

Both these famous sentences of Winston Churchill achieve emphasis of the two important thoughts—*victory* and *we shall fight*—by repetition.

Repetition is effective only when the thought emphasized is important.

RESTRICTIVE, NONRESTRICTIVE

A restrictive modifier limits the sentence element modified; a nonrestrictive modifier adds information that is *not essential* for limiting the sentence element modified. Restrictive modifiers (vital to the meaning of the sentence) are not punctuated; nonrestrictive modifiers (not vital to meaning) are set off by commas.

Restrictive   The man *who told the story* is my father.

Nonrestrictive   My father, *the man who told the story*, has lived in this area for many years.

The modifier in the first sentence is restrictive because, without it, there is no identification of the *man* under discussion: The man is my father. What man? The man *who told the story*. In the second sentence, the main statement stands without the modifier *the man who told the story*. The key to identification of *father*, the subject of the sentence, is the possessive pronoun *my*. Once we have that word, *father* is completely identified. Any further modification is nonrestrictive.

Examine this pair of sentences:

Restrictive   Two reporters *who were to cover the crime* were nationally known.

Nonrestrictive   Seth Johnson and Carl Weber, *two reporters who were to cover the crime*, were nationally known.

Since there are more than two reporters who are nationally known, the clause *who were to cover the crime* limits reporters in the first sentence. But there are only two men named Seth Johnson and Carl Weber who are nationally known. Additionally identifying them, as reporters who are to cover a crime, does not limit further. Once you have used a name in a sentence, any further modification is usually nonrestrictive. The exception occurs when a name is so common that there is a need for identification beyond that name: John Smith, William Brown, etc.

The examples given so far have been of restrictive and nonrestrictive *clauses,* but modifying *phrases* are also classified in this way and observe the same rules of punctuation.

- Henry the Eighth, King of England, married more than once.
- Mersault, the main character in Camus' *The Stranger,* appeared totally detached from life.
- The man flying the kite tripped and fell.
- The house across the street is for sale.

In the first two sentences, the modifiers are enclosed in commas, indicating that they are nonrestrictive. In the next two sentences, the absence of commas tells us that the modifiers are restrictive.

RHETORIC

The art of using language, both oral and written.

RHETORICAL QUESTION

A rhetorical question is one to which no answer is expected; it is really a statement in the form of a question. In conversation, rhetorical questions are often mocking in tone:

- If you know so much, why didn't you answer the question?

In exposition, rhetorical questions may serve as a device in argument.

> Has he not also another object, which is that they may be impoverished by payment of taxes and thus compelled to devote themselves to their daily wants and therefore less likely to conspire against him?
>
> —Plato, *Republic*

In asking this question, Plato implants the suspicion that taxation has a motive other than the support of the legitimate functions of the republic. The question is not to be answered, and Plato's statement has had its effect.

Rhetorical questions also serve as a good way to introduce a topic in the modern textbook. Read this series of rhetorical questions that opens a discussion of how to listen:

> How would you like to sit down now at a lecture for senior college students on the geological history of Outer Mongolia? How much would you learn from it—assuming you have had no previous study? How could you possibly take notes when everything the lecturer says is new for you?

The stage is set for the discussion on *listening* that follows immediately.

Such uses of rhetorical questions must not be overlooked in writing college papers. One word of warning: The effectiveness of this device can be dissipated quickly if overused.

S

SCHWA

The schwa (ə) is the symbol that represents unstressed vowels in the International Phonetic Alphabet: nick*e*l, *a*board, inf*i*nite—the italicized vowels in these three words are represented by the schwa.

SEASONS

The names of the seasons are not capitalized except in some poetry and poetic prose.

SELF

Reflexive and intensive pronouns are formed by adding *self* to the base form. As an intensive, the pronoun is used for emphasis: He *himself* will do it. As a reflexive, it frequently occupies the object position: Please *yourself* by doing what you want.

As a prefix, *self* is joined to the root word by a hyphen: self-starting, self-oriented, self-made, self-control. When *self* is the root word, no hyphen is used: selfish, selfless, selfsame.

SEMICOLON

The semicolon has two principal uses in the sentence: to join two or more independent clauses when a coordinating conjunction is not used and to separate the elements of an internally punctuated series.

Independent Clauses   When no close relationship exists between two independent clauses, a semicolon can be used to join them.

- He raced off as fast as he could; we followed at a leisurely pace.

- The trip had been interesting and enjoyable; we were all content.

A semicolon can be used along with a conjunctive adverb to join two independent clauses when a close relationship exists.

- The air was turbulent and the storm severe; nevertheless, no one seemed unduly worried.
- The politics of today bears little relationship to what we knew years ago; however, there is no doubt that the old political loyalties lie dormant.

Internally Punctuated Series When even one element of a series is internally punctuated, semicolons are used to separate the elements.

- Consider the burden of modern taxation: road taxes, which are placed on all traffic going through the town; import and export taxes; income taxes; and sales taxes.

When no element of a series is internally punctuated, commas between the elements will suffice. Although many newspapers and magazines have a tendency to omit the final comma before the last element in a series, in a formal paper that comma is retained.

- The prospectus included the title, publisher, cost, a detailed description of the program, and a list of all required materials.
- We might help him by issuing a series of commands: don't carp, don't use sarcasm, and don't shove.

SHALL, WILL

The distinctions once made between *shall* and *will* have all but disappeared. Current practice in formal writing is to use *shall* in the first person singular and plural, *will* in the second and third persons. In speech, and in general and informal writing, *will* is used in all persons.

In questions, *shall* is frequently used in the first and third persons, *will* in the second. Here again, *will* or the use of contractions frequently replaces *shall*.

- What shall we do? What'll we do?
- Shall I go? Will I go?

SHOULD, WOULD

Should and *would*—originally the past tense of *shall* and *will*—have now developed several special meanings:

1. *Should* suggests obligation, though somewhat weaker than *ought*.

- I *should* get the report done, I suppose.
- He felt that he *should* oblige her, since she had been so kind.

2. *Should* conveys a sense of uncertainty.

- The package *should* be delivered by noon if all goes well.
- The ship *should* arrive on time, weather permitting.

Should and *would* are used to state polite requests: in formal usage, *should* is used in the first person, *would* in the second and third. Usage is divided, however, and many authorities feel that *would* can be used in the first person.

- I *should* like to explain my position on this matter.
- I *would* like to explain my position on this matter.
- *Would* you please explain your position on this matter?
- *Would* the witness explain his position on this matter?

SIC

Enclosed in brackets, *sic* is used to show an error in quoted material.

- "They hoped to develope [sic] three more products."
- "We are all opposed to nucular [sic] war."

SLANG

Slang arises because language continues to grow; because occupational groups—sports writers, engineers, teachers, musicians—have to describe the same events over and over again; because cultural and ethnic subgroups constantly manufacture words and expressions that mark their users as *with it*. Often these expressions die a worthy death: *23 skidoo, that's cool, sharp*. Others persist over long periods until they become absorbed by the language: *cop* and *fuzz* for policeman, *hot dog*, *O.K.* Slang is best avoided in writing, but it can be used in dialogue if the character speaking would naturally use slang.

If slang is used when it is appropriate, do not use quotation marks around it—if the expression is right, there is no need to apologize; if it is wrong, quotation marks will not get you off the hook.

SLOW, SLOWLY

Slow was once clearly an adjective and *slowly* an adverb, but this distinction is breaking down. One commonly observes road signs exhorting motorists to DRIVE SLOW and hears fathers imploring their sons to DRIVE SLOW and STOP QUICK in case of trouble. The formal language still retains this grammatical distinction.

SO

So is both a conjunction and an intensifier. As an intensifier, *so* is rarely used in formal English.

- That play was *so* beautiful.

As a conjunction, *so* is used to introduce clauses of purpose or result.

- Ernest's reviews became increasingly unsatisfactory, *so* he was dismissed.

In formal writing, *so* is often followed by *that*.

- Booksellers decided to give less rack space to novels *so that* their profits would increase.
- He left early *so that* he could get a good seat.

In general writing, *that* is frequently omitted.

- Booksellers decided to give less rack space to novels *so* their profits would increase.
- He left early *so* he could get a good seat.

SOME

Some is both an adjective and a pronoun. As an adjective, it presents no problem for writers; as an indefinite pronoun, it can be worrisome:

- *Some* insist on leaving late.
- He ate *some* and left *some*.

Both sentences depend for their meaning on the sentences they follow. If the antecedents are clear enough, then there is no problem in either sentence. Where an antecedent is ambiguous, the sentence must be revised.

Ambiguous   Republicans and Democrats were equally enthusiastic about the chances of the candidate, but *some* were not willing to cross party lines to vote for him. (Some Democrats or some Republicans? If we have identified the candidate as a member of one of those parties, we have a chance of understanding the sentence. If we have not, then we need a divining rod.)

Revised   Both parties were enthusiastic about Jones, the Republican, but the Democrats were reluctant to cross party lines to vote for him.

All compounds containing *some* are written as one word: someone, somebody, somewhere, somewhat. If the *some* is unusually stressed, it maintains its status as a separate word: Some one, some body, etc.

SPELLING

The following list contains words frequently misspelled by the unwary. The best way to use the list is to have someone quiz you on every word. Place each word you miss on a flash card and review all your cards until you have the spellings firmly in mind. The dictionary is used over and over again by poor spellers who have to look particular words up every time they use them. If you can reduce the number of words you have to look up, you will save time that can be used to improve the quality of your writing.

Spelling List

absence	angelically	canvas
absorption	angle	canvass
accept	annual	capital
acceptance	annually	capitol
access	anxiety	carburetor
accessible	anyone (any one)	casually
accidentally	apology	category
accommodate	apologetically	cemetery
accumulate	apparatus	changeable
accustom	apparent	chaperon
achievement	appearance	chaperone (also correct)
achiever	appreciate	characteristic
acquainted	appropriate	characteristically
across	arctic	chauffeur
additionally	arguing	choose
addressed	arouse	chose
admirable	ascend	clothes
advice	assassin	colonel
advisable	athletic	colossal
advise	athletically	committee
adviser	attacked	comparative
affect	attendance	compatible
aggravate	audience	compel
aggression	bachelor	complement
aisle	balance	compliment
allege	battalion	concede
allotment	belief	conceive
all right	believe	connoisseur
allusion	benefit	conquer
a lot	benefited	conqueror
altar	benefiting	conscience
alter	boundary	conscientious
altogether	breakdown	consensus
amateur	bridal	contemptible
analogous	bridle	contemptibly
analysis	Britain	continuous
analyze	bureau	control
angel	calendar	convenience
angelic	candidate	coolly

116 [SP]

co-operate	dripping	friend
cooperate	dropped	fundamental
council	dropping	furniture
councilor	each other	genius
counselor	ecstasy	gently
courageous	eighth	ghost
courteous	embarrass	gnaw
courtesy	emphatically	government
deceit	enforce	governor
deceive	environment	grammar
decision	equipment	grief
declared	equipped	grievous
defendant	especially	guarantee
deferred	everyday (every day)	guerrilla
definite	exaggerate	guidance
dependence	exceed	handicapped
descend	excellence	handkerchief
descendant	except	hangar
describing	exhaust	height
desert	exhilarate	heinous
desiccate	existence	heroes
desirable	expense	hindrance
desiring	experience	human
desperate	facility	humane
dessert	familiar	humorous
dictionary	fascinate	hypnotize
difference	fatal	hypocrisy
dining	fault	hysterical
diphtheria	feasible	hysterically
disappear	February	imaginary
disappoint	feebly	immediately
disastrous	fiery	improvement
disease	financier	inadequate
disparate	forehead	incessantly
dispatch	foreign	incidentally
dissipate	forfeit	incredible
distribute	formally	independence
divine	formerly	indict
dormitories	fourth	indispensable
dramatically	frantically	indisputable
dripped	fraternity	indefiniteness

influence	medicine	perseverance
information	metal	persistence
ingenious	mettle	perspiration
ingenuous	miniature	persuade
initiate	mischievous	Philippines
innuendo	misspelled	physical
innumerable	misstatement	physician
inoculate	mortgage	picnic
in order	murmur	picnicking
intellectual	muscle	playwright
intelligence	mysterious	pneumonia
intercede	naive	politician
interpretative	necessary	possess
irrelevant	Negroes	possession
irreligious	nickel	possibility
irresistible	nil	precede
its	noticeable	precedent
knew	notoriety	preference
knowledge	obedient	preferred
laboratory	obstacle	preferring
legitimate	occasion	prejudice
leisure	occur	presence
let's	occurred	primitive
liable	occurrence	principal
library	occurring	principle
lieutenant	omit	privilege
lightning	omitted	procedure
livelihood	omitting	proceed
loneliness	operate	professor
loose	opportunity	program
lose	optimistic	pronunciation
mackerel	outrageous	propeller
magnificent	pamphlet	protuberance
maintain	pantomime	psychoanalyze
maintenance	parallel	psychology
manageable	parliament	publicly
manual	participate	pumpkin
manufacturer	pastime	quantity
marital	perform	quiet
marriage	permanence	quite
mathematics	permissible	quizzed

quizzes
quizzical
quizzing
receive
receipt
recommend
recurred
recurrence
recurring
reference
referendum
referred
referring
relevance
religion
Renaissance
repelled
repellent (-ant)
repelling
repetition
resemblance
reservoir
respectfully
respectively
restaurant
rhyme
rhythm
ridiculous
sacrifice
sacrilegious
salary
sandwich
scene
schedule
scissors
secretary
seize
sensitive
separate
sergeant
severely

siege
sieve
similar
sincerely
soliloquy
somewhere
sophisticated
sophomore
sovereign
specifically
specimen
stationary
stationery
statue
stature
statute
stomach
stopped
stopping
strength
subtle
subtly
succeed
success
successful
suite
superintendent
supersede
suppress
surprise
susceptible
syllable
symbol
symbolic
symbolically
symmetrical
symmetrically
temperament
temperamental
temperamentally
tendency

than-then
their-there
thorough
thousandths
till
too
tragedy
tragically
Tuesday
typical
typically
tyranny
underwent
undoubtedly
unnatural
unnaturally
unnecessary
unnecessarily
unnerving
unparalleled
unprecedented
until
usually
vacuum
vengeance
villain
visibility
warrant
warring
weather
Wednesday
weird
were-where
whether
women
writing
yacht

SPLIT INFINITIVE

The rule against splitting infinitives is as old as any of the rules that imperil writers of English. Actually, this so-called rule goes a lot further than infinitives. If it is to be followed at all, the rule should be *do not split any verb form!* The reason usually given for this rule is that split verbs are not good style, which is no reason at all. The proper reasons for not splitting verb forms are: (1) your reader may not understand what you mean, and (2) split verbs frequently are awkward. Thus, if splitting improves understanding and is not awkward, it is permissible to split infinitives or any other verb form.

> *Poor* Many generations of Americans *have* under the threat of war *seen fit* to take up arms and fight.
>
> *Improved* Under the threat of war, many generations of Americans *have seen fit* to take up arms and fight.
>
> *Poor* Would you care *to,* if you have the time, *go* with me to the store?
>
> *Improved* If you have the time, would you care *to go* with me to the store?

The matter of splitting verb forms, then, depends on how you care to split them. If the interrupting element is long, splitting will not improve understanding and will be awkward.

SPOONFUL

Such words as *spoonful, cupful* and *shovelful* form their plurals by adding *s: spoonfuls, cupfuls, shovelfuls.* These words are measures of quantity rather than numbers of spoons, cups, or shovels filled with something or other. To say *three spoons full of milk* would mean that you have three full spoons in front of you waiting to be spilled. *Three spoonfuls* would be an appropriate expression for a recipe. In speech one hears these forms used alternatively, but the distinction between them should be retained in writing.

STYLE

Judgments of style are concerned with considering how well the words and patterns of words a writer uses contribute to his purpose in writing, whether that purpose is to inform, argue, explain, intrigue, entertain, or uplift. George Orwell cited six rules for style that he felt would be helpful when the instinct for the right word or the right construction fails:

> 1. Never use a metaphor, simile, or other figure of speech which you are used to seeing in print.
>
> 2. Never use a long word where a short one will do.
>
> 3. If it is possible to cut a word out, always cut it out.
>
> 4. Never use the passive where you can use the active.
>
> 5. Never use a foreign phrase, a scientific word or a jargon word if you can think of an everyday English equivalent.
>
> 6. Break any of these rules sooner than say anything outright barbarous.
>
> —George Orwell, "Politics and the English Language"

Orwell was not writing about literary English, but about language as an instrument for expressing thought. For Orwell, then, style meant aptness of expression, or how a concept is stated.

No one can teach a person style in six easy lessons. Style is individual and goes deeply into the personality of the writer. What must be done is to encourage every writer to develop his own style, and the teacher can do no more or no less than point out aspects of a writer's style that appear good—or bad—to the teacher.

Yet if Orwell can give six rules for style, it is also worthwhile to give six pointers on style that the authors of this book try to follow:

> 1. Determine before you write what audience you are writing for; this will give your writing direction, determine the appropriate level of diction, and help settle the question of how deeply you will investigate the subject of your paper.
>
> 2. Try always to put the logical subject of every sentence in the subject position; this will work handily with Orwell's fourth rule.
>
> 3. Find the most precise verb for every sentence you write. Avoid verbs that require modifiers in order to approach the degree of precision you want to achieve.
>
> 4. If you use figurative language, examine it to determine whether it is consistent and fresh and whether it adds to meaning.

5. Evaluate your diction. Is it all of the same level, is it precise, does it convey your intended meaning? The dictionary and thesaurus will help.

6. Write whatever you want to write early enough so that you can put it away for a period of time and then go over it when you are fresh and have time to evaluate how well you have conveyed your ideas. Check particularly all adjectives and adverbs to determine whether they can be eliminated.

SUBJECT

The subject of a sentence is the word or group of words that stands in a precise relationship to the verb—the element that performs the action expressed by the verb, or the word that receives the action of a passive verb. The subject controls the person and number of the verb. Writers who separate subject from verb by too many words risk violating the rules of agreement, but even when they are lucky enough to get the agreement straight, they usually leave their readers wondering who did what to whom in the sentence.

SUBJECTIVE COMPLEMENT

A predicate nominative and predicate adjective are both subjective complements of a linking verb.

- She seems *happy* in her work. (predicate adjective)
- John felt *maudlin.* (predicate adjective)
- He was a *doctor.* (predicate nominative)
- They were *assassins.* (predicate nominative)

Complements complete linking verbs. Omit a complement and your sentence will say nothing: She seems. John felt. He was. They were.

SUBJUNCTIVE MOOD

Largely discarded in English, the subjunctive mood persists in these uses:

Condition Contrary to Fact

- If I *were* the leader of this group, I would make sure our meetings ran in a more orderly fashion.
- *Were* I twenty years younger than I am, I might have a chance of capturing the attention of undergraduates.

Verbs of Asking, Recommending, etc. In formal English, the subjunctive is used in *that* clauses after verbs of asking, demanding, suggesting, etc.

- The judge recommends that the plaintiff *withdraw* his suit.
- The committee requests that the interested member *confine* his remarks to the proper issue.

General English would avoid these uses of the subjunctive by substituting the infinitive.

- The judge urges the plaintiff *to withdraw* his suit.
- The committee requests the interested member *to confine* his remarks to the proper issue.

The writer who is in doubt about the use of the subjunctive would do best to avoid it. Time is on his side. Even formal English will discard it one day.

SUBORDINATING CONJUNCTION

A subordinating conjunction connects a subordinate clause to a main clause or to another subordinate clause. The most frequently used subordinating conjunctions are the relatives: *who, which, what,* and *that.* Others are *because, since, as, as if, so, when, where, why,* and *how.*

SUBORDINATION

Subordination is the stylistic practice used to give modifying units the degree of emphasis appropriate to their importance. These modifying units range from single words to lengthy subordinate clauses. *Proper* subordination enables the reader to focus his attention on the important concepts in writing; *improper* subordination hinders rather than aids meaning. In many cases improper subordination results from carelessness in editing.

> *Improper*   A boycott of the school was conducted by parents. The parents demanded that educational standards be maintained.
>
> *Proper*   The parents boycotted the school, demanding that educational standards be maintained.

Proper subordination was achieved by eliminating the unnecessary repetition of *parents* and changing the verb *demanded* into the verbal modifier *demanding*. In the process, the passive verb *was conducted* became *boycotted*, an active verb, and the logical subject *parents* moved into the subject position.

Another mistake in subordination can occur if prepositional phrases are piled upon one another: *the demands of the parents* can become *parents' demands* or *parental demands; the wallpaper in the living room* can become *the living room wallpaper*.

SUBSTANTIVE

A substantive is a word or group of words that performs a noun function.

SUCH

As an intensifier, *such* is appropriate to informal English, but not to formal English.

- This was *such* a bad play.
- They found him *such* a bore.

Empty intensifiers diminish intensity rather than increase it. Without *such*, the two examples state the case simply and dramatically.

- This was a bad play.
- They found him a bore.

Note that the changed sentences do not specify *why*, but neither did the originals. Perhaps we should not permit value judgments without a full statement of charges and complete evidence. At any rate, adding *such* did not make the original statements truer or clearer or more emphatic.

Several formal English constructions employ *such*, but they are generally awkward and should be avoided:

- Their attitude was *such* that the other members of the committee felt obliged to issue a dissent.
- The weather was *such* that the air control tower decided to shut down the airport.

Such in both sentences implies a situation that forces action, but it does not specify what the situation is. It would be better to write:

- The majority report erred in several major sections, so the other members of the committee felt obliged to issue a dissent.
- The rain was so heavy that the air control tower decided to shut down the airport.

SUFFIX

A suffix is an element added to a root or word to make a new word: compos*er* enclose, enclo*sure*. Suffixes and prefixes together are called *affixes*.

SYNTAX

Syntax is the grammatical relationship among units of a sentence. Proper syntax keeps meaning clear, while poor syntax leaves readers guessing.

T

TENSE

Tense is the characteristic of verbs that tells the time in which the verbs operate. There are three simple tenses (present, past, future) and three perfect tenses (present perfect, past perfect, and future perfect). Except for the simple present and the simple past, most tenses in English are formed with the use of auxiliaries, the principal one being *have*.

Present The present tense is used to express present actions, future actions, habitual actions, and conditions true for all time.

- He *is* too sick to see you.
- The ship *sails* at noon tomorrow.
- He *rides* to work every day.
- All roads *lead* to Rome.

Past The past tense expresses actions completed in the past.

- John *walked* twelve miles last Wednesday.
- The wind *blew* the house down.
- That road *led* to Rome.

Future The future is expressed by the simple form of the verb with *will* or *shall*. The confusion that has existed over the use of these two auxiliaries has been resolved in colloquial English and largely in general English, both of which now use *will* exclusively. In general and formal English, *shall* is used for the first person singular and plural, and *will* is used for second and third persons singular and plural. In speech the problem is avoided by use of contracted forms: *we'll, I'll, you'll, he'll*, etc.

The future tense can also be indicated by various idiomatic constructions:

- I am *going to* leave on the 9:45.
- New York City is *about to* require new license plates.

- Professor Donner *is to give* the course next year.

Present Perfect   The present perfect indicates that an action begun in the past continues in the present.

- John *has worked* at his job for eight years.
- Oregon *has* long *been* a scenic state.

Past Perfect   The past perfect distinguishes between the times of two past actions by indicating time prior to past time:

- Deirdre *had worked* at perfecting her ballet form for five years before she finally achieved a satisfactory performance.
- Bob *had collected* unemployment insurance for almost three months before he found work.

Future Perfect   The future perfect expresses time prior to another future time. The present or future tense is used with the future perfect.

- The virus *will have taken* hundreds of lives before a satisfactory cure is found. (The future time is expressed here by the present *is found.*)
- The virus *will have taken* hundreds of lives before a satisfactory cure will be found.

Progressive tenses are also available for action in progress. These tenses use the present participle with appropriate auxiliaries:

- How long *have* you *been dieting*?
- I thought you *had been dieting* much longer than three weeks.
- I *will have been dieting* for most of my life if I live less than ten more years. (Notice that the future is expressed by the present *live.*)

The problem of tense can be complicated endlessly, as the foregoing discussion demonstrated. Remember that tense makes distinctions in time. If there is no need to complicate relationships that are clearly defined, do not complicate them. Examine the tenses used by Ernest Hemingway to see how simple a matter tense can be in the hands of a skilled writer.

THAN

Than is both a conjunction and a preposition.

Conjunction   As a conjunction, *than* introduces clauses of comparison.

- The need for inspection was greater *than* either man had realized.
- The pony was taller *than* Jody. (In this sentence the clause of comparison is implied: The pony was taller than Jody was.)

This kind of construction is called *elliptical*. The significance of such a construction is understood only when a pronoun follows *than*. The pronoun takes its case from the function of the pronoun in the elliptical clause.

- The pony was taller *than he*. (In this sentence the implied clause of comparison has *he* as its subject: The pony was taller *than he was*.)
- He sees you more often *than me*. (The clause of comparison has *me* as its object: He sees you more often *than he sees me*.)

Preposition   As a preposition, *than* demands the objective case.

- He knows no one *than whom* he is fonder.

Of course, this construction is extremely awkward and should be avoided.

In colloquial English, *than* usually takes the objective case.

- Wilt is taller *than him.*
- Elsie is fatter *than her.*

General and formal English use the subjective. *Than* in both of the following sentences is a conjunction, not a preposition:

- Wilt is taller *than he* [is].
- Elsie is fatter *than she* [is].

THAT

That is used as a conjunction, relative pronoun, demonstrative adjective, and adverb.

Conjunction. *That* is used most frequently as a conjunction introducing an object clause after verbs of seeming, believing, hoping, wishing, and the like.

- All of us hoped *that he could go.*
- John hoped *that the operation would be delayed.*

In formal English *that* is never omitted before such clauses, but in general English it frequently is.

- All of us hoped *he would go.*
- John hoped *the operation would be delayed.*

When more than one *that* clause is used, *that* is repeated before each clause to emphasize the parallel structure and so improve clarity.

- All of us hoped *that* he could go and *that* he could stay for at least one month.
- John hoped *that* the operation would be delayed, *that* another treatment could be found, and *that* he would lose no more time from work.

That is also used in restrictive clauses.

- The summer home *that* interested him had been sold. (The distinction between using *that* and *which* in nonrestrictive clauses is losing ground, but in formal writing this distinction should be retained.)

Relative Pronoun As a relative pronoun, *that* refers to persons or things, *who* to persons, and *which* to things.

- The book *that* pleases me most year after year is *Portrait of the Artist as a Young Man.*
- A man *that* (or *who*) works hard usually succeeds.

Demonstrative Adjective As a demonstrative adjective, *that* indicates or emphasizes choice.

- *that* boy, *that* book, *that* house
- Did you think I meant *that* house?

Adverb   *That* functions as an adverb in structures such as:

- We were not there *that* long.
- As long as you were willing to work *that* hard, you might at least have taken the time to plan your work.

THEN

Then is an adverb of time and is also used as a conjunctive adverb:

- We *then* went on to debate the issue for four hours.
- Dick worked out for two hours; *then,* tired by his efforts, he lay down in the shadow of the stadium.

Then must not be confused with *than.*

THERE IS, THERE ARE

In the common constructions *there is* and *there are, there* may be called an anticipatory subject. The word that performs the subject function follows the verb. In this type of construction, the verb takes its number from the functional subject, not from *there.*

- There *is* a tavern in the town.
- There *are* many taverns in East Rutherford.

When the subject is compound and the first element of the compound subject is singular, the verb is singular.

- There *is* too much cream and sugar in that coffee for my taste.

When the first element of the compound subject is plural, the verb is plural.

- There *are* forks and a napkin in that drawer.

Turning any of the above *there is, there are* constructions about will resolve problems of number:

- Too much cream and sugar *is* in that coffee for my taste.
- Forks and a napkin *are* in that drawer.

There is and *there are*—and their stylistic cousin *it is*—delay the arrival of the functional subject, so overuse of these terms leads to flat, poorly styled writing. How often do you use these constructions? If you want to tighten your writing and make it more emphatic, determine how many *there* and *it* structures you can eliminate the next time you write.

THING

The word *thing* is so abstract and indefinite that it frequently has no meaning in a sentence. It is classified as deadwood. In the following sentence, see how *things* is used:

- One of the most important *things* in life is living it.

What does *things* mean? The sentence can be rewritten in at least two different forms:

- Living is one of the most important aspects of life.
- One of the most important aspects of life is living it.

Notice that in the first rewrite, *living* is given the greatest prominence by assigning it the subject position; in the second, *one* occupies the subject position. If the thought we are discussing were part of a paragraph, the focus of the paragraph would determine which of the two approaches we would use. One cannot imagine a paragraph pattern in which *one of the most important things* would be preferred in the subject position of this sentence.

Thing is but one example of deadwood; all deadwood must be pruned if you are to become an effective writer.

TITLE

Underscore the titles of books, magazines, newspapers, and long poems. Use quotation marks for titles of articles, essays that appear in books, short stories that are part of collections, and short poems. Usage is divided on the titles of poems, but in formal writing it is best to underscore. Do not underscore or use quotation marks for titles of book chapters or for a preface or introduction.

The rule for capitalizing titles is arbitrary enough to please all: use capitals for all words except articles and prepositions of less than five letters, and capitalize the first and last words of the title.

- *Major Barbara*
- *The Taming of the Shrew*
- *A Funny Thing Happened on the Way to the Forum*

Theme Title   Every paper submitted to a teacher should have a title, and the best time to write a title is after the theme has been completed. The quality of a title is judged by its appropriateness—does it give the reader a good idea of what he will find in the paper? If you read a paper through carefully before writing the title, you will have a better appreciation of what the paper will say to an objective reader. Cleverness has no place in title writing if cleverness obscures meaning in any way.

TO, TOO, TWO

Is carelessness to blame for the fact that *to, too,* and *two* are so often misspelled in college themes?

TRANSITIVE AND INTRANSITIVE VERBS

A verb is transitive when it takes an object, intransitive when it does not. Many verbs, like *prove,* can be both transitive and intransitive:

- He proved the problem.
- He proved wrong in his assertion.

TRANSPOSE

Transpose ($\sim$) is a frequently used correction mark that indicates that elements in a sentence or paragraph should be moved to improve clarity or emphasis.

TRITE

Trite, worn-out words and phrases are to be avoided in a paper. Avoid any phrases you are used to seeing in print: *on the spur of moment, by hook or by crook, stiff as a board.*

U

UPPER CASE

Upper-case letters are capital letters; lower-case letters are small letters.

USAGE

When a teacher or editor uses the word *usage,* he is indicating that the marked passage departs from standard English usage. In the case of a word so marked, check your dictionary. In the case of a larger element, determine whether all the parts are in order.

V

VERB

A verb is a word or group of words that indicates the relationship between the subject and object if there is one. It indicates the action or state of the subject.

VERBAL

Verbals are derived from verbs. There are four forms of verbals: the present participle (looking), the past participle (looked), the infinitive (to look), and the gerund (looking). The present and past participles are used as adjectives. The infinitive is used as a noun or adjective. The gerund is used as a noun. Verbals take objects and may be modified adverbially.

Present Participle
The *winning* team played hard.
Past Participle
The *unharmed* bird flew away.
Infinitive
To play seemed more important than *to win.* (noun)
He gave me some honey *to eat.* (adjective)
Gerund
He likes *swimming.* (object)
Sliding on the ice is fun. (subject)
He was good at *swimming.* (Object of preposition)

Although verbals have the appearance of verbs, they do not function as verbs.

VERB-ADVERB COMBINATIONS

Often an adverb completes the meaning of a verb or is used in combination with the verb to form a new verb. Treat the combination as a verb when the combination has a meaning that is altogether different from the literal meanings of the two separate words.

- *Look up* the side of the house. (verb and adverb)
- *Look* eleemosynary *up* in the dictionary. (verb)

VERY

Very is an intensifier that has been so overworked that it is of little value. Find a better intensifier or use a stronger word. Under no circumstances should you use *very* with a superlative: *very best, very least,* etc.

VOICE

Voice is that aspect of a verb that indicates the relationship of a subject to the action described by its verb. *Active* voice indicates that the subject is performing the action of the verb; *passive* voice indicates that the subject is acted upon.

Active   The car *rammed* the stone wall.

Passive   The stone wall *was rammed* by the car.

Active   The student *opened* his book at last.

Passive   The book *was opened* at last by the student.

The passive is formed by compounding some form of the verb *to be* with the past participle. When the passive is used, the grammatical subject position is occupied by the logical object, and the logical subject is relegated to a prepositional phrase or is omitted entirely.

- The carpenter *drove* the final nail into the coffin.

In this sentence, the subject *carpenter* is performing the action. If we wish to emphasize *nail*, the logical object, we can place it in the subject position and change the construction into a passive:

- The final nail *was driven* into the coffin by the carpenter.

We can give further emphasis to *nail* by omitting the logical subject *carpenter* entirely:

- The final nail was driven into the coffin.

The proper use of the passive depends on whether we achieve additional emphasis through its use. The following example shows again how the writer changes the point of view of the reader by changing from active to passive:

- Dempsey knocked Firpo out of the ring.
- Firpo was knocked out of the ring.

In this example, the writer has a stylistic choice between the active and passive; is he trying to tell what *Dempsey* did or what happened to *Firpo?*

One characteristic of dull writing is excessive reliance on passive constructions. Use the passive only when the logical object is to be emphasized.

W

WHERE

In addition to its use as an interrogative pronoun (*Where* are you going?), *where* is used to introduce adjective clauses indicating place.

- I would like to know of a ski area where no one has broken a leg.

Where is also used to introduce adverbial clauses.

- Look where you are driving. The tree lay where it was felled.

Where is not used to describe a process.

Incorrect   Pitching is where you throw the ball to the catcher.
Correct   Pitching means throwing a ball to the catcher.

WHICH

Which is used to refer to things, not people.

Incorrect   The clerk to which you gave the message is absent.
Correct   The clerk to whom you gave the message is absent.

Which is used to introduce nonrestrictive clauses.

- The 1966 session of Congress, which enacted some useful legislation, had many freshman members.

Which should never be used as a catchall to refer to anything that precedes it. There is a sensible limit to the amount of verbiage a reader can be expected to remember.

- He decided to explain the situation to the policeman once more even though he thought he had explained it all adequately in the first three attempts, which was not in agreement with the facts. (*What* was not in agreement with the facts?)

[WH]

In reading transcripts of press conferences of important political figures, we see this naive reliance on *which* and wonder what was meant by the pronoun. Strangely enough, those who attend such conferences usually are able to understand what is meant. The requirements of clear writing are much more rigorous than the requirements of speech.

WHO, WHOM, WHOSE

Who is the subjective form of the pronoun, *whom* the objective, *whose* the possessive. We confuse these forms in our writing because we use them carelessly in conversation.

Incorrect   Who are you thinking of?
Correct   Whom are you thinking of?
Correct   Of whom are you thinking?

In these examples, the problem of *who* and *whom* develops when the preposition *of* is separated from the pronoun. Another pronoun problem develops when the relative pronoun precedes the verb even though the pronoun is the object of the verb:

Incorrect   No matter *who* you trust, you are sure to be cheated if you are not careful.

Correct   No matter *whom* you trust, you are sure to be cheated if you are not careful.

When *who* is the subject of a relative clause, the verb takes its number from the antecedent of *who.*

• He is one of the few *teachers who take* their vacations in the fall. (The verb *take* is plural because *who* refers to *teachers:* Of the teachers who take their vacations in the fall, he is one.)

• Al is one of those *lawyers who are* willing to help their clients even if their clients are not rich.

Choosing between *who* and *whom* can be troublesome in clauses that have a relative pronoun as subject or object. As a way out of the difficulty, substitute the personal pronoun to determine whether you want *who* or *whom.*

- I shall give the money to the man *whom* I designated. (I designated *him.*)
- The nominee will be the man *who* gets the most votes in the primary. (*He* gets the most votes.)
- The student *who* she says was with her that day could not be located. (The pronoun *who* is the subject of *was*, not the object of *says*. *She says* is a parenthetic expression that does not affect the pronoun *who*.)
- The man *whom* he found asleep in the cabin had no right to be there. (He found *him* asleep in the cabin.)

WORDINESS

How many words can you eliminate from your writing without hurting the essential meaning? (If you know the number, then you will improve your writing.) Many writers of another day appear to have believed that long sentences lent elegance to style, but modern writers would rather be succinct. Redundant expressions, excessive use of the passive, and deadwood make for wordiness. Examine these sentences:

Wordy Minorities have been working toward the goal of achieving full civil rights.

Improved Minorities have been working to achieve full civil rights.

Wordy Putting aside the fact that their children had been told what the rules are, we may yet say that the Browns neglected their children in many ways.

Improved The Browns told their children the rules, but neglected them in other ways.

This kind of editing contributes to clarity by eliminating unnecessary words and subordinating unimportant ideas. Further, the passive verb in the second example has been replaced by an active verb and this contributes to the strength of the revision. Finally, *the fact that* is always a good candidate for the red pencil, along with *it seems that, it should be noted that, it was here that,* and their stylistic cousins.

Y

YOUR, YOU'RE

Your is the possessive, *you're* the contraction.

- *Your* car is waiting, sir.
- *You're* going to find that college is much different from high school.

Catalog

If you are interested in a list of fine Paperback
books, covering a wide range of subjects
and interests, send your name and address,
requesting your free catalog, to:

McGraw-Hill Paperbacks
1221 Avenue of Americas
New York, N.Y. 10020